WAYNESBURG COLLEGE LIBRARY
WAYNESBURG, PA.

327.7291   G942u
Guggenheim, Harry Frank
The United States and Cuba
85265

FEB 24 '79

THE UNITED STATES AND CUBA

The United States and Cuba

A Study In International Relations

By

HARRY F. GUGGENHEIM

Select Bibliographies Reprint Series

BOOKS FOR LIBRARIES PRESS
FREEPORT, NEW YORK

First Published 1934
Reprinted 1969

STANDARD BOOK NUMBER:
8369-5127-1

LIBRARY OF CONGRESS CATALOG CARD NUMBER:
78-102242

PRINTED IN THE UNITED STATES OF AMERICA

To
MY WIFE
and
Our Embassy Family at Havana

"Mientras más amigos, más claros."

ACKNOWLEDGMENT

WHILE the responsibility for the opinions in this book is entirely my own, I wish to acknowledge my indebtedness to all those who have contributed to the background of information required for its preparation. I am especially grateful to those Cuban and American friends in Cuba, the memory of whose sympathetic understanding and warm hospitality I shall always cherish, and to my loyal and splendid staff at Havana. The staff was under the able direction of Edward L. Reed, first Secretary of the Embassy, and included for a period, in addition to the official personnel, Dr. Philip C. Jessup, as personal legal adviser, who contributed much to this book, especially by his admirable study of precedents under the Permanent Treaty; his successor for another period, Mr. Edgar Turlington, who contributed especially by his surveys of pardons, amnesties and electoral laws; and Mr. Grosvenor Jones, who acted for a period as personal economic adviser, and made invaluable studies of financial and economic subjects. Later Albert Nufer, Commercial Attaché, and his expert staff ably supplemented these reports. I give my warm thanks to Mr. Burnham Carter, private secretary during my entire stay at Havana, who has laboriously read all of the manuscript for this book and has made many valuable suggestions. My thanks are also due to Miss Florence P. Spofford, who has verified citations, and to Mrs. Bertha Richards Kendig for her collation and copying of important documents.

Acknowledgment is made to the Cuban Government and Department of State of the United States Government for permission to publish some hitherto unpublished documents, and to the Historical Adviser, Dr. Hunter Miller, and the Chief of the Division of Research and Publication, Dr. Cyril Wynne, for their kind coöperation. Research for this book was greatly aided by the use of the comprehensive facilities of the Library of Congress under the courteous and skilled direction of the librarian, Mr. Herbert Putnam, and his associates.

FOREWORD

THIS book is a review of United States relations with Cuba, briefly tracing the development of this relationship since Spanish colonial times. It is a study of the effects of the Platt Amendment which has governed these relations since 1902, and makes definite recommendations to modify the Treaty in which the Amendment is incorporated.

The book does not attempt to tell the story of the four years 1929–1933 while I was in Havana. Those years were dramatic in the extreme—perhaps the four most turbulent years in Cuba's republican history. But because the events of those years are so close at hand and I was so intimately connected with them, it would not seem fitting for me to undertake a critical appraisal of the policies and personalities of the period.

My acquaintance with Cuba began as early as 1907 when I stopped there on my way to a three-year mining apprenticeship in Mexico. Subsequently I visited the island at various times on trips to and from mining undertakings in other Latin American countries. I have never had any business interest, directly or indirectly, in Cuba. When I retired from business in 1923, later to assume the Presidency of the Daniel Guggenheim Fund for the Promotion of Aeronautics, my interest in the Latin American countries continued to find expression through service on various international commissions. My acquaintance with Cuba deepened into an enduring affection as I learned to know the island well in my official residence there for four years.

The island lies long and narrow in the mouth of the Gulf of Mexico almost midway between Mexico and the United States. Only about ninety-five miles of sea separate Cuba and the United States at their closest point of proximity. The island is about seven hundred and thirty miles long and averages about fifty miles in width. The coast line, guarded by innumerable chains of islets and coral keys, is dotted with magnificent harbors.

Months of travel over a country's surface fail to give the vivid general impression that is presented by a survey from the air. The first impression of Cuba from an airplane is that of a country of stately royal palms with graceful green crests beautifying every panorama; then that of a vast fertile plain set out in yellow patches of sugar cane which wave and glisten under a sun, blazing from a very clear blue and white sky. But this impression must be later altered to include the mountain ranges, covered with dense forests of superb hardwood and running cascade brooks, and

FOREWORD

the sandy and marshy low lands, and great fresh water swamps, haunts of the crocodile and wild fowl.

Nature is both bountiful and cruel to Cuba. The country abounds in bird and reptile life with the venomous snake unknown, and is noticeably lacking in wild mammalia. The shore waters and estuaries harbor quantities of various highly colored fishes, molluscs and crustaceans, and also the curious manatee or sea cow which suckles its young. The tropical heat and humidity provide an abundance of alimentary plants and delicious fruits. As many as three crops of potatoes, for example, can be harvested in a year, and some nutritious vegetables ripen within thirty days after the sowing of the seeds. Bananas grow year after year from the same root stock with little or no cultivation. The royal palm provides all materials needed for a *bohio*—the countryman's hut of Indian origin. The tree's trunk provides wood for siding, and its leaves, thatch for roofing. In the warm Cuban climate man requires little clothing and no fuel for heating.

However, this Arcadian existence is at times violently interrupted when the summer hurricanes sweeping across the Caribbean occasionally strike parts of Cuba, carrying crops and shelters before them and leaving devastation in their wake.

The winter climate of Cuba is delightful. From November to April is the so-called "dry season"; but during these months, unlike the continuous dry spells of many countries, there are some rainy days to break the monotony and to water a soil already moistened by heavy early morning dews. In the summer the Cuban night always brings refreshment from the burning sun; the narrow island is then swept by breezes from the sea filling the soft air with perfume of flowers and moist earth. The blue of the night sky —almost as blue as the incomparable sky of Madrid —is studded with the brilliant stars of the tropics.

When Columbus came to Cuba, he found a primitive race of Indians scattered over the island whom Las Casas called Siboneyes, and a less primitive race of Tainan Arawak of peaceable habits "as contrasted with the warlike and cannibalistic Carib"[1] of neighboring islands. Little is known of these Cuban aborigines. Supposedly they were exterminated within fifty years, perishing under the Spanish sword or the equally fatal Spanish policy of working them in mines and fields. Today one rarely finds any trace of Indian blood in the features or characteristics of the Cuban, such as is so frequently noticeable in certain other Latin American peoples. The introduction of the negro slave to replace the exterminated Indian has, however, left its imprint on Cuba as it has on the south of the United States.

The Spanish pioneers, noting Cuba's agricultural wealth and strategic position, soon made the island

[1] M. R. Harrington, "Cuba before Columbus" in *Indian Notes and Monograph*, N. Y., 1921, Vol. II, p. 413.

FOREWORD

an important center for expeditions of discovery and conquest, and for buccaneering and slave trading. They brought to the New World a form of the feudal system, the marks of which linger today in Cuba in the landlordism, extremes of riches and poverty, lack of education and of self-reliance in the masses. The more superficial manifestations are found in wrought iron gates and crumbling stone walls outlining spacious verandas, picturesque patios, slave compounds —once the lovely country seats of lords of local communities. The ruins of these old sugar and coffee plantations, with lengthy and grand approaches usually marked by four majestic rows of royal palms, still indicate some of the wealth of the days when fortunes were measured by the thousands of slaves a man owned. The old city of Havana has the stamp of feudal Spain in its fortresses, convents and palaces, many of which in beauty of line, color and texture lend distinction to the architecture of the New World. In contrast is the new Havana with its bright streets, modern shops and hotels, cool cafés and white beaches which offer so strong an appeal to the thousands of travellers who in normal times visit Cuban shores in winter.

Cuba's population has been recently recorded at nearly four millions; a little less than sixty per cent. of the inhabitants are the descendants of the Spanish settlers with some admixture of other blood; a little more than thirty per cent. consist of people of negro and mixed blood; and the remaining ten per cent. are foreign born, principally Spanish.

The large negro and mixed population constitutes a difficult social problem which has been met in a different manner from that adopted in the southern section of the United States. In Cuba this part of the population has the franchise in fact as well as in theory, and on account of its lack of education and preparation for democratic government contributes largely to political instability. Away from Havana and the larger cities, the white and black races mingle freely and easily. In Cuba are found at one end of the negro scale of civilization, a primitive laboring class, descendants of African tribes, some surreptitiously practising *ñañigismo*, a relic of barbarism similar to voodooism; and at the other end of the scale where there has been an infiltration of white blood, energetic farmers, some brilliant soldiers, politicians and alert students contributing to the country's development.

In Havana and other cities the social lines are strictly drawn by that part of the population which is descended from the inhabitants of feudal Spain. This class struggling to maintain against modern forces the culture and dignity peculiar to other days adds the charm and grace that are delightfully characteristic of the life of Cuba's *alta sociedad* or high society.

In the white portion of the population are many *guajiros* or farmers, usually tenant farmers. They

FOREWORD

are shrewd, hard-working, self-respecting, splendid citizens. In their development perhaps lies the future hope of Cuba.

The population is widely scattered over the countryside and in towns of small size. There are few large cities, other than Havana, situated on the western end of the island with a population of nearly six hundred thousand; and Santiago on the eastern end, with a population of nearly one hundred and fifty thousand. A recently constructed modern boulevard runs through the center of the island connecting these cities and passes through great cattle ranches and through land producing sugar, tobacco, pineapples, henequin, coffee, cereals, vegetables and fruits.

Havana, the center of politics, finance, and industry, is the great show window of Cuba. But the island's vitality, its real beauty, and its great possibilities lie in the Cuban countryside beyond.

At a luncheon at the Havana Yacht Club, I recalled, in a farewell address, some of those characteristics of Cuba which are the endearing features of a country so closely related to the United States:

"The rhythm of your folksongs; the curiously powerful and pervasive smell of sugar during the *zafra;* the thatched roof of a *bohio* guarded by royal palms; the clear, warm mornings and the breeze that rises in the evenings—all these are aspects of Cuba that will remain in my remembrance and which have perhaps been emphasized by the very harshness of the events through which the world has passed.

"What I have just said is an effort to indicate the graciousness of nature in Cuba. I should add that that is paralleled by the graciousness of the nature of the Cubans. I had long known of your reputation for kindness and hospitality; I have found that reputation more than confirmed by my experience. It has not been lessened by economic stringency; it has been indeed the more remarkable because of it. In the city or in the country the Cuban has set a high standard for all civilized peoples in his treatment of his guest. In my trips through the countryside of Cuba I have frequently been amazed at the kindness accorded us by people who had nothing to spare, and yet who spared it. It was a hospitality in penury which I shall not forget. Nor is it a hospitality of food and shelter only, but a hospitality of things that are not material as well—a generosity of humor, a keen, light wit, a cheeriness that helps to dispel the *lacrimae rerum* of the times."

H. F. G.

Falaise,
Port Washington, Long Island.
April 1933–April 1934.

CONTENTS

	PAGE
FOREWORD	ix

PART I
UNITED STATES RELATIONS WITH COLONIAL CUBA ... 1

PART II
FORMATION OF TREATY RELATIONSHIP BETWEEN THE UNITED STATES AND THE CUBAN REPUBLIC ... 47

PART III
THE INFLUENCE OF THE UNITED STATES ON ECONOMIC DEVELOPMENT IN CUBA ... 110

PART IV
POLITICAL ACTIVITIES IN CUBA AND THEIR RELATION TO UNITED STATES POLICY ... 155

PART V
UNSATISFACTORY EVOLUTION OF THE RELATIONSHIP UNDER THE PERMANENT TREATY ... 192

PART VI
REVISION OF THE TREATIES ... 235

SELECTED BIBLIOGRAPHY ... 251

THE UNITED STATES AND CUBA

PART I

UNITED STATES RELATIONS WITH COLONIAL CUBA

THROUGHOUT the history of the United States Cuba has occupied a place of peculiar, if unrecognized importance in our foreign affairs. No other country has so continuously concerned our Department of State.

Following the struggle of the original states for survival and protection, the Monroe Doctrine established the basic principle of our foreign relations, and in the development of this policy Cuba played a highly important rôle. Similarly Cuba has been an important factor in the development of our international trade, and the restrictions which Spain imposed upon our trade with Cuba greatly influenced our attitude toward the Spanish Government and hence toward its Cuban colony. In addition, Cuba was a factor in the development of our policy of territorial expansion. When our country was torn by the issue of slave territory, Cuba was one of the lands in bitter dispute. When we became a united formidable nation, tempted by the urge of empire, our "manifest destiny" involved us in Cuba. And finally in the stage

THE UNITED STATES AND CUBA

of our mammoth economic expansion we have penetrated the island of Cuba with our wealth as we have no other country of the world.

Cuba, "the pearl of the Antilles," was a jewel coveted by statesmen of the Old World to adorn many a royal crown long before the brilliance of its lustre dazzled the eye of no less a democrat than Thomas Jefferson, who said of it:

> "I have ever looked on Cuba as the most interesting addition which could ever be made to our system of States. . . . Her addition to our confederacy is exactly what is wanting to advance our power as a nation to the point of its utmost interest." [1]

In addition to this acquisitive interest in Cuba characteristic of statesmen of that epoch, there was real concern that Cuba in the wrong hands might imperil the interests of our country. As Madison expressed it, some power "might make a fulcrum of that position against the commerce and security of the United States."

There is little doubt that the promulgation of the Monroe Doctrine was a product of early nineteenth century American political thinking which found much inspiration in the history and political possibilities of the island of Cuba. The initial pronouncement by President Monroe was contained in his message to

[1] Paul L. Ford, *Writings of Thomas Jefferson*, N. Y., 1899, Vol. X, pp. 261, 278.

Congress on December 2, 1823. This document, fundamental to American foreign policy, read in part as follows:

" . . . the occasion has been judged proper for asserting, as a principle in which the rights and interests of the United States are involved, that the American continents, by the free and independent condition which they have assumed and maintain, are henceforth not to be considered as subjects for future colonization by any European powers. . . .

"We owe it, therefore, to candour, and to the amicable relations existing between the United States and those powers to declare that we should consider any attempt on their part to extend their system to any portion of this hemisphere as dangerous to our peace and safety. With the existing colonies or dependencies of any European power we have not interfered and shall not interfere. But with the Governments who have declared their independence and maintained it, and whose independence we have on great consideration and on just principles acknowledged, we could not view any interposition for the purpose of oppressing them, or controlling in any other manner their destiny, by any European power in any other light than as the manifestation of an unfriendly disposition toward the United States." [2]

It is interesting to note that in the previous April Secretary of State John Quincy Adams, author of the document, wrote in an instruction to Hugh Nelson, American Minister to Spain, the following:

"These islands [Cuba and Puerto Rico] . . . are natural

[2] James D. Richardson, *Messages and Papers of the Presidents*, N. Y., 1897–1927, Vol. II, pp. 778, 787.

appendages to the North American continent; and one of them, Cuba, almost in sight of our shores, from a multitude of considerations has become an object of transcendent importance to the commercial and political interests of our Union . . . there are laws of political as well as of physical gravitation; and if an apple severed by the tempest from its native tree cannot choose but fall to the ground, Cuba, forcibly disjoined from its own unnatural connection with Spain, and incapable of self-support, can gravitate only towards the North American Union, which by the same law of nature cannot cast her off from its bosom. . . . The transfer of Cuba to Great Britain would be an event unpropitious to the interests of this Union. . . . The question both of our right and of our power to prevent it, if necessary, by force, already obtrudes itself upon our councils, and the administration is called upon, in the performance of its duties to the nation, at least to use all the means within its competency to guard against and forefend it." [3]

Throughout the first half of the nineteenth century our Department of State was continuously concerned lest Cuba fall from the weaker hands of Spain into the stronger hands of either France or England as she had fallen a prey to the latter with the aid of American colonial troops for one year from 1762 to 1763. When John Quincy Adams became President, his Secretary of State, Henry Clay, instructed the chiefs of our missions in the principal European capitals that we "could not consent to the occupation of these islands [Cuba and Puerto Rico] by any other Eu-

[3] W. C. Ford, *Writings of John Q. Adams*, N. Y., 1917, Vol. VII, pp. 372, 373, 379.

ropean power than Spain under any contingency whatever."

This fear of foreign interference was not unjustified. After our purchase of the Floridas in 1819, for example, a press campaign was carried on in England insisting that steps be taken at once to carry out a much discussed plan for the cession of Cuba by Spain to England. It was required "as a depot of thunder" to awe the United States. The fact that Spain was hard-pressed for funds to carry on the Carlist wars lent credence to reports from time to time that Spain would sell Cuba to England or France, or would cede the island temporarily as security for a loan. In 1836 the Queen of Spain actually sent an agent to Talleyrand to propose the sale of Cuba, the Philippines and Puerto Rico to Louis Philippe. The contract was drawn and presented to the French King; but at the last moment, perhaps foreseeing England's resentment at this secret sale, Louis declared the price was too high and pushed the paper across the table, remarking that unless there was a reduction, the contract might as well be thrown into the fire. The Spanish envoy, personally opposed to the sale, promptly threw the document into the flames, somewhat to Louis's astonishment.[4]

Such incidents led to the idea of a joint agreement among the interested powers in regard to Cuba. As

[4] *Vide* James M. Callahan, *Cuba and International Relations*, Baltimore, 1899, pp. 173-174.

early as 1823, when the United States Government feared that Cuba might fall into Britain's hands, consideration was given to a policy of coöperation between the United States and other nations concerning Cuba. In that year England proposed to the United States that they pursue a joint policy toward the Spanish American colonies, but the United States rejected the idea because it resembled an "entangling alliance."

In 1825 Canning proposed that France, the United States and England should disclaim any intention of occupying Cuba and should protest against such occupation by others. France, after encouraging the idea at first, rejected the proposal. This facilitated Clay's refusal on behalf of the United States. Clay stated, however, that after the friendly communication between England and the United States on the subject "each must now be considered as much bound to a course of forbearance and abstinence in regard to Cuba and Puerto Rico as if they had pledged themselves to it by a solemn act." At the same time he wrote to the American Minister in Paris instructing him to say to the French Government that he could not suppose that any European power would occupy the island without the concurrence or knowledge of the United States.

In addition to this constant fear of European aggression in Cuba, the United States was concerned lest the newly formed Spanish American republics should create a situation in Cuba inimical to American interests. The new Republics of Colombia and Mexico were particularly active in their endeavors to expel Spain completely from the Western hemisphere. They plotted to incite Cuba to rebellion and, failing in this, prepared to send armed expeditions to the island. These expeditions were abandoned (reluctantly by Mexico) under the pressure of notes from Henry Clay.

At the same time, in 1826, the first Pan-American Conference was held at Panama through the efforts of Simón Bolivar with the objects of forming a league of states to resist Spain, of protecting the newly formed republics from European aggression, and of promoting the liberation of Cuba and Puerto Rico. President John Quincy Adams accepted the invitation to this conference, but with the understanding that the delegates of the United States would not be authorized to act in any way inconsistent with the neutral attitude of their country toward Spain and her rebellious colonies. Due to attacks on the administration by both the Senate and House for participation in this conference, the delegates were delayed in reaching Panama, and arrived after the conference had adjourned—a failure.

. . . . .

As the slave question became acute in the middle of the nineteenth century it affected our relations with Cuba; first, because of the slave trade; second, because of the South's desire to extend slave territory; and third, on account of the Abolitionists' desire to end slavery. The annexation of Texas in 1845 and the acquisition of more Mexican territory in 1848 and 1853 were results of our expansionist policy which did not overlook the possibilities of the annexation of Cuba.

In addition to this sectional controversy over slave territory there had been numerous controversies over the slave trade into Cuba. In 1814 the United States and Great Britain by the Treaty of Ghent agreed to do all in their power to extinguish the traffic in slaves, but not until 1842, by the Webster-Ashburton Treaty, did the United States join in the maintenance of squadrons off the west coast of Africa to accomplish this purpose effectively. In the interim slave traders used the American flag to escape search, a practice which resulted in unpleasant diplomatic incidents, some of which were of Cuban origin.

At various periods during the latter part of the nineteenth century, there were even fears of the establishment of a black republic in Cuba. In 1841 the population of Cuba consisted of 571,129 free persons and 436,497 slaves. In spite of the anti-slave trade treaties, it was estimated that about 25,000 negroes were entering Cuba each year. Webster caused an investigation to be made in both Cuba and Spain of Britain's alleged designs of "converting the government into a black military republic under British protection." In 1851 Lord Palmerston went so far as to instruct the British Ambassador at Madrid to say to the Spanish Minister for Foreign Affairs that if steps were provided for the emancipation of slaves in Cuba it would tend to "create a most powerful element of resistance to any scheme for the annexation to the United States."

These apprehensions were among the reasons which had led President James K. Polk, three years before, to instruct his Secretary of State, James Buchanan, to attempt the purchase of Cuba. Spain was unwilling to consider any proposals to relinquish possession of "the ever faithful isle", the principal remnant of its once great American empire.

From this time on, various plans were devised in the United States on behalf of Cuban independence, or annexation to the United States. Beginning in 1849 General Narciso López organized the first of three filibustering expeditions thought to be supported by the great Creole slave-owners who wished to put themselves under the protection of the American slave-holding system. The South responded generously to General López' appeals for aid, and even New York, as indicated particularly in the metropolitan newspapers, was sympathetic to his undertaking.

In order to fulfill his international obligations, disregarding the Southern sympathy for the Cuban revolution, President Zachary Taylor on August 11,

1849, issued through Secretary of State, John M. Clayton, a proclamation by which he warned "all citizens of the United States who shall connect themselves with an enterprise so grossly in violation of our laws and treaty obligations, that they will thereby subject themselves to the heavy penalties denounced against them by our acts of Congress, and will forfeit their claim to the protection of their country." He further admonished his countrymen that "an enterprise to invade the territories of a friendly nation, set on foot and prosecuted within the limits of the United States, is in the highest degree criminal." [5]

This proclamation was extremely unpopular in the South, since the Cuban question was now becoming a sectional and political issue. The ebb and flow of political tides have carried our Cuban problem back and forth and have interfered with that more profound current of sound national policy that should uninterruptedly carry such an international problem on its course.

The ships of the first López expedition were seized by United States Government agents while preparing to set out for Cuba. The second expedition reached Cárdenas, but López, contrary to his expectations, did not find the Cubans ready to rally to his support. After an engagement with the Spaniards, he was forced to reëmbark and return to the United States.

[5] James D. Richardson, *op. cit.*, Vol. VI, p. 2545.

RELATIONS WITH COLONIAL CUBA

When remnants of his force landed at Key West, the United States authorities thought it inadvisable to make any arrests in view of the popular enthusiasm for the Cubans' cause. Spain promptly demanded, in the following indignant terms, that appropriate action be taken against this violation of international law:

> "If contrary to our expectations the authors of this last expedition should go unpunished, as did those who last year planned the Round Island expedition, the Government of Her Majesty will find itself obliged to appeal to the sentiments of morality and good faith of the nations of Europe to oppose the entrance of a system of politics and of doctrines which would put an end to the foundations on which rests the peace of the civilized world. If Europe should sanction by her silence and acquiescence the scandalous state of affairs by which the citizens of the United States (or those of any power whatever) might freely make war from their territory against Spain, when the latter is at perfect peace officially with the Union; if it should be tolerated or looked on with indifference that the solemn stipulations which bind the two states should be with impunity made hollow by mobs and that the laws of nations and public morality should be violated without other motive than the selfishness of the aggressors, and with no other reliance than force, then civilized nations ought to renounce that peace which is based on the laws of nations and the terms of treaties and make ready for a new era in which might will be right, and in which popular passions of the worst kind will be substituted for the reason of states." [6]

[6] Willis F. Johnson, *The History of Cuba*, N. Y., 1920, Vol. III, pp. 59-60.

This protest could not be ignored, and López and a number of his followers were arrested and indicted. However, it was almost impossible to obtain evidence against them and after the disagreement of three juries, the indictments were finally dismissed. The prisoners were liberated, and López prepared and launched his third expedition, consisting of some four hundred men, most of whom were Americans. This expedition was routed by the Spaniards in Cuba, and López and fifty of his followers were executed.

The expedition caused a profound impression in both America and Europe. It brought the Cuban question closer to the minds and hearts of the general public in the United States than it had been heretofore. In England and France it caused apprehension lest the ripening Cuban apple should soon fall into the outstretched hands of Uncle Sam. The fear was expressed in England that should Cuba be seized by the United States to satisfy southern pro-slavery expansionists, Canada would then be coveted by northern abolitionists to provide additional free soil to keep the Union scale in balance.

Perhaps impelled by the same fear, the Spanish Government again persuaded England in 1852 to attempt to obtain a declaration on the part of France, the United States and England, guaranteeing Cuba to Spain. In a lengthy diplomatic correspondence in which Daniel Webster and Edward Everett, both Secretaries of State under President Fillmore, took part, the United States refused to enter into such a pact, in spite of Spain's threat that in case of our refusal, it was her desire that England and France should declare that they never would allow any other power, at any time, to possess itself of "Cuba, either by cession, alienation, conquest or insurrection of the same."

In a postscript to a personal letter Secretary Everett referred to this important Cuban matter as follows:

"I have in a very long, and (for me) bold letter to the English and French ministers declined to join their Governments in a tripartite guaranty of Cuba, disclaiming, however, all purpose to appropriate it to ourselves. . . ." [7]

The reason for this position was explained in a subsequent note from Everett to the American ministers in France and England. After affirming the American attitude toward the acquisition of Cuba by any European power, he wrote:

"The President does not covet the acquisition of Cuba for the United States; at the same time, he considers the condition of Cuba as mainly an American question. The proposed convention proceeds on a different principle. It assumes that the United States have no other or greater interest in the question than France or England; whereas it is only necessary to cast one's eye on the map to see how

[7] Foster Stearns, "Edward Everett," in *American Secretaries of State*, Vol. VI, p. 124.

remote are the relations of Europe, and how intimate those of the United States, with this island." [8]

President Fillmore's administration was not sufficiently aggressive for the leaders of the Democratic Party who correctly sensed the exuberance of the American people at this period for their "manifest destiny". "The platform managers of those who soared under the label of 'Democracy', advertised and prophesied a brilliant foreign policy. They said the young republic had reached the tide in her affairs when she could grasp the opportunity to bury 'fogyism', reform the navy, brush the cobwebs from the stars and stripes, and let her light shine from the tops of her commercial craft to diffuse knowledge and freedom unto all lands." [9]

In his message of 1852 the President, however, merely called attention to the inconvenience of our commercial relations with Cuba. From the beginning of her colonial history Spain had regulated commerce with her colonies on the basis of restrictive measures designed to benefit herself. Colonial trade was largely confined to Spain, and for a period during the seventeenth century trade with any other country, in accordance with prevalent European theory, was an offence which carried the penalty of death to the offender and the confiscation of the property involved. Spain imposed heavy duties on foreign ves-

[8] *Ibid.*, pp. 129-130.
[9] James M. Callahan, *op. cit.*, p. 239.

RELATIONS WITH COLONIAL CUBA 15

sels entering Cuba; despite American protests she did not lighten them. The United States was continually irritated by being hampered in its efforts to trade with an island so near its shores. Notwithstanding these inconveniences, however, Fillmore considered that Cuba's incorporation into the Union would be "fraught with serious peril" on account of the character of its people and the danger of affecting the industrial interests of the South.

With the election of Pierce and a new Democratic administration, the attitude toward Cuba became less indifferent. In his inaugural address President Pierce declared that "our attitude as a nation and our position on the globe render the acquisition of certain possessions, not within our jurisdiction, eminently important for our protection, if not in the future essential for the preservation of the rights of commerce and peace of the world."

The new administration plunged into the Cuban question at once by appointing as diplomatic representatives to Spain, England and France three men—Pierre Soulé, James Buchanan and John Y. Mason respectively—who were all in favor of the acquisition of Cuba. Soulé's appointment was made with some concern that Spain might withhold the *agréation* on account of his views, which he had freely expressed in the Senate, favoring the acquisition of Cuba "but not by purchase", and his commendation of filibustering. The misgivings with respect to the suitability of

16 THE UNITED STATES AND CUBA

the appointment were deepened by the circumstances of Soulé's departure for Spain.

When Soulé embarked at New York en route to that country, the Cuban junta—the revolutionary committee—in New York "determined to stage a demonstration which should serve both as a farewell to the new Minister to Spain, and as a rally for their cause of Cuban freedom".[10] After a torch light parade in Soulé's honor, the leader of the junta uttered a discourse in which he closed with the hope "that on your returning home, a new star shining in the sky of Young America may shed its dawning rays upon your noble brow".[11]

Soulé's acceptance of this farewell demonstration was a diplomatic blunder and his speech in response an insult to the Government to which he was accredited, for which he was properly rebuked by Secretary of State Marcy. In responding, Soulé had said: ". . . . The American Minister ceases not to be an American citizen, and, as such, has a right to carry wherever he goes the throbbings of that people that speak out such tremendous truths to the tyrants of the old continent." [12]

This was the strange beginning of a strange diplomatic career. There was at least nothing dull about Soulé, not even in appearance. As a contemporary de-

---

[10] A. A. Ettinger, *The Mission to Spain of Pierre Soulé*, New Haven, 1932, p. 174.
[11] *Ibid.*, pp. 175-176.
[12] *Ibid.*, p. 176.

RELATIONS WITH COLONIAL CUBA 17

scribed him, " 'the black velvet clothes, richly embroidered, the black stockings, a black chapeau, and a black dress sword, set off his black eyes, black locks, and a pale complexion, and gave him a striking appearance. He looked indeed, not like the philosopher whose costume he imitated, but rather like the Master of Ravenswood.' " [13]

Secretary Marcy's first instructions to Soulé were to arrange a commercial treaty with Spain which would enable the American Government to deal directly with the Captain General of Cuba. Marcy considered the time inopportune to attempt to purchase the island. Later, on April 3, 1854, he authorized Soulé to negotiate a sale of Cuba for a maximum price of $130,000,000. If he failed in this, Marcy wrote, "you will then direct your efforts to the next desirable object which is to detach that island from the Spanish dominion and from all dependence on any European power".[14]

In the meanwhile, an international incident was developing which nearly fixed the date of the Spanish American War over Cuba at 1854 instead of 1898. This concerned the *Black Warrior*, an American steamer plying between Mobile and New York and stopping at Havana for passengers and mail. Although over thirty trips had been made by the steamer to Havana, shipments not billed to Cuba had

[13] *Ibid.*, p. 223.
[14] *Ibid.*, p. 247.

never been entered in the manifest. This was an irregularity accepted by usage. On a trip at the end of February, 1854, a cargo of cotton was carried *in transitu* and as usual not recorded. The port authorities protested the irregularity, refused the agent the privilege of correcting the manifest, confiscated the cargo and arrested the captain.

Soulé, who had accomplished nothing in his mission to Madrid except to increase his unpopularity by wounding the French Ambassador to Spain, the Marquis de Turgot, in an unwarranted duel, seized upon the *Black Warrior* affair as an occasion for unauthorized representations with a hope of gaining Cuba by intimidation. However, in the course of the long negotiations, Soulé was informed that President Pierce was "unwilling to resort to any extreme measures". After Soulé's mission was terminated, the Spanish Government remitted the fine that had been imposed upon the owners of the *Black Warrior* and paid an indemnity agreeable to the United States Government.

In the interim President Pierce, much concerned with the Cuban problem, thought that a joint conference of his Ministers to England, France and Spain "might possibly result in something favorable to our negotiations with Spain". It did result in the preparation by them at Ostend, under the watchful eye of the secret police of France, of the amazing "Ostend Manifesto" (Oct. 18, 1854), which provoked a European indictment of American diplomacy as "cer-

RELATIONS WITH COLONIAL CUBA 19

tainly a very singular profession, which combines with the utmost publicity the habitual pursuit of dishonourable objects by clandestine means".[15]

The manifesto was in the form of a report to Secretary Marcy. It recommended that every effort should be made to purchase Cuba. It undertook to show that the United States must annex Cuba in order to have peace with Spain and to preserve the Union. It pointed out the advantages to Spain from such a sale which would provide funds for paying debts and building railroads. Then anticipating the possible refusal of Spain to sell even though the solicitous diplomats predicted that by selling "Spain would speedily become what a bountiful Providence intended she should be, one of the first nations of Continental Europe—rich, powerful and contented", they argued: "Self-preservation is the first law of nature, with states as well as with individuals", and "After we shall have offered Spain a price for Cuba far beyond its present value, and this shall have been refused, it will then be time to consider the question, does Cuba in the possession of Spain seriously endanger our internal peace and the existence of our cherished Union. Should this question be answered in the affirmative, then, by every law human and divine, we shall be justified in wresting it from Spain, if we possess the power." [16]

[15] *Ibid.*, p. 407.
[16] *Ibid.*, pp. 363-364.

By the time this report reached Marcy, however, the latter was apparently regretting his instructions that we must "detach that island from the Spanish dominion". The political passions aroused by the Kansas-Nebraska Act which placed the slave-expansionist and abolitionist issues squarely before the American people decided Cuba's fate in the Pierce administration. Through the passage of the Act the northern abolitionists were aroused to the point of violent opposition to the annexation of any more slave territory. In a letter to a friend a little later, Marcy wrote: "I am entirely opposed to getting up a war for the purpose of seizing Cuba . . . The robber doctrine I abhor. If carried out, it would degrade us in our own estimation and disgrace us in the eyes of the civilized world . . . Cuba would be a very desirable possession, if it came to us in the right way, but we cannot afford to get it by robbery or theft."

This attitude prevailed in the lengthy discussions which President Pierce held with his cabinet. The Administration decided to repudiate the "Ostend Manifesto", and Soulé was calmly advised that Marcy refused to admit the inference that the Ministers at Ostend had counseled a policy of seizure. In this way, Marcy effectively, if somewhat awkwardly, extracted the charge from this diplomatic bomb. "Obviously," said Marcy's biographer, "there was no man able or strong enough to guide this particular phase of our foreign affairs in a straightforward and high-

RELATIONS WITH COLONIAL CUBA

minded way. Politics, sectional strife, and animosity over the domestic issue of slavery were at the bottom of the mismanagement of the phase." [17]

Despite the criticism of this whole affair, Buchanan, one of the authors of the "Ostend Manifesto", was nominated for the Presidency by a southern democracy grateful for his efforts at Ostend to add new slave territory to the nation. After his election he kept faith by pursuing the project to purchase Cuba. In 1859 a bill was introduced in Congress to provide a sum of $30,000,000, to be placed at the disposal of the President, so that he might have something in hand with which to bargain with Spain. There was great opposition to the bill, and it was finally tabled.

In the following year a group in the Democratic Party bolted from Douglas and nominated John C. Breckinridge of Kentucky for the Presidency on a pro-slavery platform which included a demand for the annexation of Cuba. But the split in the party was fatal to its chances and gave the office to Abraham Lincoln.

It was characteristic that the Civil War should also involve the question of Cuba—although one might think that the little island would be far removed from such a conflict. Both the North and the South, however, were soliciting Spanish sympathy. The

[17] H. Barrett Learned, "William Learned Marcy," in *American Secretaries of State*, Vol. VI, p. 216.

American Chargé d'Affaires at Madrid reported to Secretary Seward, "I showed the government of Spain, by speeches pronounced in South Carolina, Georgia, and Louisiana at the breaking out of the rebellion, that its leaders already, leaping beyond the eventualities of the war against the federal government, were holding up to the population of the south the plan of immediately annexing Cuba, Santo Domingo, and Mexico, as one of the grand results to be attained by severing their connexion with the north".[18]

On the other side Secretary of State Benjamin of the Confederacy wrote to Slidell, his special commissioner at Madrid, that the Confederacy would not annex Cuba and authorized him to agree to guarantee Cuba to Spain, if necessary to the success of his mission.

Nothing came of these efforts to disturb Spain's neutrality and with the termination of the war and the preservation of the Union, both of the two dominant considerations shaping our Cuban policy were eliminated. First, Cuba had been a constant source of anxiety to our statesmen lest it fall into the hands of some strong foreign power to jeopardize our security or to hinder our national aspirations. Second, it had become involved in the controversy over slave territory. The Civil War put an end to the slavery ques-

[18] *U. S. Papers Relating to Foreign Affairs, 1861–62*, Washington, 1862, Part II, p. 515.

tion, and our country emerged as a powerful, unified nation, defiant of foreign aggression.

. . . . .

The Cuban issue now began to be pressed very vigorously by the Cubans themselves. President Grant's two terms from 1869 to 1877 nearly coincided with the ten years war in Cuba from 1868 to 1878, during which Cuba's troubles were a constant source of irritation and injury to the United States and which prepared public opinion for the Spanish American War.

The ten years war began with the announcement of Cuban independence in October, 1868 by the patriot Carlos Manuel de Céspedes and his followers. And a few months later these Cuban leaders established the Republic of Cuba with a declaration of independence claiming "that Spain governs the Island of Cuba with an iron and blood-stained hand. The former holds the latter deprived of political, civil, and religious liberty." A provisional government was organized under Céspedes, the head and spirit of the movement, whose first decree was an emancipation proclamation. As soon as Grant was inaugurated, the Cuban revolutionists addressed an appeal to him for recognition:

"Because from the hearts of nineteen-twentieths of the inhabitants of the island go up prayers for the success of the armies of the republic; and from the sole and only want of arms and ammunition these patient people are kept under the tyrannical yoke of Spain.

Because the republic has armies numbering over 70,000 men actually in the field and doing duty. . . .

Because the United States is the nearest civilized nation to Cuba, whose political institutions strike a responsive chord in the hearts of all Cubans. The commercial and financial interests of the two peoples being largely identical and reciprocal in their natures, Cuba earnestly appeals for the unquestionable right of recognition. . . ." [19]

Walter Millis gives an ironic contrast to this description. He says:

"The Ten Years' War . . . was not a great popular uprising. It rarely got beyond the stage of irregular guerilla fighting in the wild, unsettled regions at the eastern end of the island. It never penetrated the rich and populous west, where the real strength of the island was centered about the capital at Havana. Its principal support was a Cuban junta at New York—active in the established departments of propaganda, collections and gun-running—and its chief leader in the field was General Máximo Gómez, a Santo Domingan. But it kept military revolt alive in Cuba for a decade and, like the López expeditions before it, it awoke the immediate attention of the United States." [20]

Although Grant's personal sympathies were with the Cubans, he was counseled to refrain from recognizing them. The United States was not in a bellicose

---

[19] Willis F. Johnson, *op. cit.*, Vol. III, pp. 200-201.
[20] Walter Millis, *The Martial Spirit*, Boston, 1931, p. 13.

mood. Among other reasons influencing this decision was the fact that Great Britain's recognition of Confederate belligerency in 1861 was again being assailed by American political leaders who in 1869 were seeking a settlement of the *Alabama* claims.

However, American rights and interests were being disregarded by Spanish authorities in Cuba. Secretary of State Fish protested to the Spanish Minister, López Roberts, frankly admitting that "there pervades the whole American people a special desire to see the right of self-government established in every region of the American hemisphere, so that the political destiny of America shall be independent of transatlantic control." [21]

Secretary Fish instructed General Sickles, Minister to Spain, to propose the use of the good offices of the United States to end the "civil war" in Cuba on the basis of Cuban independence and the abolition of slavery, and to give the Spanish Government to understand that if the conflict continued "an early recognition of belligerent rights is the logical deduction from the present proposal".

The efforts at mediation came to nothing, and the insurrection, as it continued, provided causes of irritation for both the United States and Spain. From time to time, expeditions were organized in the United States by the Cuban junta to aid in the rebel-

[21] U. S. Department of State, *Correspondence*, H. R. Ex. Doc., No. 160, 41st Congress, 2d Sess., p. 81.

lion; and bands of American soldiers of fortune, adventurers and mercenaries, supplied with arms and ammunition from the United States, ran the Spanish blockade. Spain was frequently indignant at these minor violations of the neutrality laws; and the United States on its part felt itself injured by the embargo of American property in the Cuban colony and by the trial of American citizens there by courtmartial when Spain had not recognized the existence of a state of war in Cuba. The barbarity of the fighting on both sides scandalized the feelings of the American people and resulted in loss of American life and property on the island. The United States was able to obtain little satisfaction from Spain on account of these injuries. In October, 1873, Fish in a despatch to Sickles remarked: "I must frankly say that the present state of things cannot last. Our patience and endurance are sorely tried."

The famous case of the *Virginius* illustrates the grievances of both countries. The *Virginius* incident was the forerunner of many conspiracies between Cubans and United States citizens to carry on illicit and even criminal acts under the protection of the United States flag, much to the embarrassment of the United States Government. Under United States registry and with a mainly United States crew, the *Virginius* had a record of various revolutionary activities in both Venezuela and Cuba in 1871. When pressed too

RELATIONS WITH COLONIAL CUBA 27

closely by Spanish pursuers, it had obtained the escort of United States warships.

In 1873, however, the boat was captured by a Spanish cruiser on the high seas between Jamaica and Cuba and taken into Santiago. It carried a large cargo of arms and a party of revolutionists. The Spanish authorities promptly executed fifty-three of the men taken on board; and ninety-three others were saved only by the intervention of a British cruiser which happened to come into port and the outraged commander of which threatened to bombard the city if any more English or United States citizens were executed in so summary a fashion. The drumhead court-martial was a barbarity, which Fish characterized, under the pressure of highly inflamed public talk of war, as "butchery and murder". He sent a telegram to Sickles stating: "If Spain cannot redress the outrages perpetrated in her name in Cuba, the United States will." Fish demanded in an ultimatum the release of the ship, and of the surviving prisoners, a salute to the United States flag, and the punishment of those responsible for the executions.

The Spanish Government was conciliatory, but wanted the facts of the case established. Fish eventually carried the incident to conclusion through Admiral Polo, the Spanish Minister to Washington, who offered primarily the immediate release of the ship and men. The Attorney General of the United States decided that the *Virginius* was not entitled to sail under the United States flag, toward which the Spanish Government disclaimed any intention of indignity. The salute was dispensed with, but a year later under great pressure Spain paid $80,000 to the United States Government for the lives of those executed at Santiago.

In the complexity of the situation Fish was driven by "pressure from various interested and sympathetic quarters in favour of intervention on behalf of the Cuban insurgents" to an expedient which was in opposition to the basic principle of United States foreign policy, the Monroe Doctrine. Fish instructed our ministers in six foreign capitals to urge these governments to counsel Spain to settle the controversy in Cuba in order to avoid an intervention by the United States. He sent an instruction to Caleb Cushing, who had replaced Sickles at Madrid, stating the President "feels that the time is at hand when it may be the duty of other governments to intervene ... He will, therefore, feel it his duty ... to submit the subject in this light ... for the consideration of Congress." [22]

Much to Fish's surprise, the European powers were not interested in his proposal; their attitude was summed up in Lord Derby's reply in which he said to the American Minister that he was "willing ... to co-operate in any way that promised to bring about a

[22] U. S. Department of State, *Correspondence*, Cuba, Ex. Doc. No. 90, p. 11.

RELATIONS WITH COLONIAL CUBA

settlement of troubles in Cuba, but is not prepared to put any pressure on the Spanish Government or to put forward proposals which he has reason to think it would not be inclined to accede to".[23] The contemplated American intervention and the approach to the European powers were fully aired in the press of Europe and the United States much to Fish's embarrassment. He was even called upon by the Democratic House of Representatives to communicate the correspondence on this subject.

. . . . .

With the end of Spain's internal troubles on the Península in 1876, that country actively engaged to stamp out the Cuban insurrection, which nevertheless dragged along wearily for another two years. In December, 1877, President Hayes said in his message: "We suffer, but abstain from intervention". In the following February, the ten years war came to an end with the peace treaty of Zanjón, and the United States had its longest respite—nearly twenty years—from its eternal Cuban problem. The Treaty of Zanjón gave to Cuba theoretical representation in government and provided for a gradual emancipation of the slaves, but not until 1886 was slavery actually abolished in Cuba.

In spite of Cuban hopes from the Treaty of Zanjón

---

[23] Joseph V. Fuller, "Hamilton Fish," in *American Secretaries of State*, Vol. VII, p. 198.

and the lessons of the ten years war, Spain continued to exploit Cuba in the traditional manner for her own benefit. The restrictions placed on Cuba's trade on behalf of the mother country were the cause of diplomatic protests by the United States. These, and the ensuing effort to negotiate trade treaties, and the spasmodic threat of renewed revolutionary activities kept the Cuban question alive in the United States. Cuban annexation was still frequently discussed in the halls of Congress and even in the Department of State; until in February, 1895, in the little village of Baire, the so-called *grito de Baire,* the shout or battle cry, proclaimed the final Cuban war for independence.

This time the shout had considerable volume, and if it was not heard round the world, the Cuban junta in New York amplified its tones to such an extent that it was certainly heard all round the Americas.

The time for the revolution was well chosen, because the depression of 1893 had crushed Cuba as general depressions always do and as only a one-crop country can be crushed. In addition, the Wilson Tariff restoring the duties on Cuban sugar was enacted in 1894 which aggravated Cuba's plight and exacerbated the spirit of discontent.

The conflict between Spain and Cuba was an orgy of pillage and destruction on both sides. José Martí, the acknowledged father of the Cuban revolution, was betrayed and shot in ambush by the Spaniards, and thereafter the revolutionary policy degenerated into an effort to ruin Cuba, on the theory that if the Spaniards would not give up the island, then it should be made worthless to them. Like the Cuban *alacran*, the scorpion which according to legend lifts its poisonous tail to its own head when hopelessly trapped, and injects the death sting, the Cuban revolutionists attempted the utter destruction of the island. The Spaniards under the newly appointed Captain General Weyler retorted in kind with his much advertised *reconcentrado* policy. Cuban men, women and children were driven from the land and collected in huge concentration camps under the eyes of Spanish garrisons. The effect of both the Spanish and Cuban policy was ruin to the country, disease, starvation and death to the inhabitants. The life and property of United States citizens did not escape.

From the beginning the sympathy of the United States was with the Cubans in this final effort. In September, 1896, Secretary Olney reported to President Cleveland that the revolution "was just in itself, commanding the sympathy, if not the open support, of the great bulk of the population affected, and capable of issuing in an established, constitutional government".[24] These ethical reasons for sympathy were supplemented by economic considerations. As the revolu-

---

[24] Montgomery Schuyler, "Richard Olney," in *American Secretaries of State*, Vol. VIII, p. 287.

tion progressed, claims for destruction of American life and property piled up in the Department of State, as well as protests from Spain against the infraction of the neutrality laws.

The forces acting upon the American mass mind, finally exploding with the *Maine,* have been neatly catalogued by James Truslow Adams as follows:

"An idealism in the people at large that could be easily aroused in favour of any people supposed to be oppressed and struggling for freedom; a really bad and difficult situation in Cuba; a group of powerful business men and politicians bent on imperial expansion; a group of newspapers callously searching for sensational news which could be translated into circulation; and a shining new gun in our hands of which we were proud." [25]

After long and bitter debates in the House and Senate of the United States, a joint resolution was passed recognizing the insurgents, and tendering the good offices of the United States for a settlement of the war on the basis of the independence of Cuba. This resolution was ignored by President Cleveland, and under his direction Secretary of State Olney sent a note to the Spanish Minister to Washington, Dupuy de Lôme, not insisting on independence, but tendering the good offices of the United States for composing the conflict on the basis of liberal reforms in the Government of Cuba. And then Olney added:

[25] *The March of Democracy,* 1933, Vol. 2, p. 249.

RELATIONS WITH COLONIAL CUBA 33

"On all these grounds and in all these ways the interest of the United States in the existing situation in Cuba yields in extent only to that of Spain herself, and has led many good and honest persons to insist that intervention to terminate the conflict is the immediate and imperative duty of the United States. . . . The United States has no designs upon Cuba and no designs against the sovereignty of Spain. . . . Its geographical proximity and all the considerations above detailed compel it to be interested in the solution of the Cuban problem whether it will or no." [26]

The Spanish Government made no direct reply to this offer of good offices, but Dupuy de Lôme answered the note diplomatically by showing why, due to the Cubans, there could be no success from mediation.

In President Cleveland's last message to Congress in 1896 he said:

"I have deemed it not amiss to remind the Congress that a time may arrive when a correct policy and care for our interests, as well as a regard for the interests of other nations and their citizens, joined by considerations of humanity and a desire to see a rich and fertile country intimately related to us saved from complete devastation, will constrain our Government to such action as will subserve the interests thus involved and at the same time promise to Cuba and its inhabitants an opportunity to enjoy the blessings of peace . . ." [27]

[26] Montgomery Schuyler, "Richard Olney," *American Secretaries of State*, Vol. VIII, p. 288.
[27] James D. Richardson, *op. cit.*, Vol. XIII, p. 6154.

Millis' account of the reaction of Congress to this message and of the country to the events of this period is illuminating:

"Congress met on December 7, and listened to Mr. Cleveland's message with an apathy broken only during the reading of the Cuban passages. Though cold, as ever, to the aspirations of Cuba Libre, Mr. Cleveland went further in the direction of intervention than he had ever gone before. The nation was in an expectant mood; the propagandists were redoubling their efforts, there was war talk in the air. But almost as the words were being read, a Spanish column in Havana Province was blundering into a party of mounted Cubans. There was a burst of rifle fire; and when the confusion was over, Antonio Maceo, the outstanding figure in the insurrection, was lying dead upon the ground. He had abandoned the remnant of his forces in Pinar del Río, and, slipping out with a small escort, was making his own escape to the eastward when his party was accidentally intercepted.

"For a moment it was enough to stagger even the propagandists themselves, and for the first day or two all they could do was to deny the news *in toto* as a Spanish fabrication. But then they recovered; they rose to the occasion and revealed the full measure of their ability. A Mr. J. A. Huau, of Jacksonville, Florida, a Cuban-American said to be of Chinese extraction, informed the reporters that he had just received a 'private letter' from Cuba. It 'confirmed' the news that Maceo was dead, but added, he said, that the general had been lured forth by a flag of truce and brutally assassinated by a Spanish soldiery too cowardly to meet him in fair fight. At once the northward-going wires were hot

RELATIONS WITH COLONIAL CUBA 35

with this outrage. It created a sensation—but the sensation was favourable to the Cuban cause." [28]

President McKinley rode into office on a Republican platform that capitalized the Cuban situation by inserting a plank stating that since Spain had "lost control of Cuba" and was "unable to protect the property or lives of resident American citizens", the government of the United States "should actively use its influence and good offices to restore peace and give independence to the Island."

In his first annual message, December 6, 1897, McKinley referred to the reconcentration policy saying: "It was not civilized warfare. It was extermination." And in considering the course for the United States to take, he said: "I speak not of forcible annexation, for that can not be thought of. That, by our code of morality, would be criminal aggression".[29]

McKinley was politically opposed to an intervention in Cuba which would mean war with Spain, but he drifted into it. Upon his assumption of office the Cuban question was relatively quiescent. The Spanish Government had proposed reforms for Cuba which had been favorably received in the United States. Diplomatic claims between the United States and Cuba were being settled. McKinley made a final effort to solve the problem by the purchase of the

[28] Walter Millis, *op. cit.*, p. 61.
[29] James D. Richardson, *op. cit.*, Vol. XIII, pp. 6256, 6258.

island, but his negotiator, Whitelaw Reid, was given to understand that Spain would not be interested in such a proposal.

With regard to the Cuban rebellion, the McKinley administration made its first formal statement in a note to the Spanish Minister in June, 1897, in which Secretary of State Sherman declared:

"Against these phases of the conflict, against this deliberate infliction of suffering on innocent noncombatants, against such resort to instrumentalities condemned by the voice of humane civilization, against the cruel employment of fire and famine to accomplish by uncertain indirection what the military arm seems powerless to directly accomplish, the President is constrained to protest, in the name of the American people and in the name of common humanity." [30]

To this Dupuy de Lôme replied pointedly as follows:

"If the American people, to whose philanthropic sentiments reference is made in Your Excellency's note of June 26, understood, from a dispassionate examination of this question, that the insurrection lives for evil only, and, instead of encouraging it by holding out the fallacious hope of assistance, which is the basis of all its trust, would counsel peace; if, instead of aiding and abetting the violations of law which are constantly committed by the Cuban emigrants organized here for the purpose of making war upon a nation friendly to the United States, they would aid the Fed-

[30] U. S. *Foreign Relations, 1897;* p. 508.

RELATIONS WITH COLONIAL CUBA 37

eral Government in its efforts to prevent the departure of the filibustering expeditions which render this long and desolating war possible, all the evils would very soon cease which are deplored by His Majesty's Government and by all Spaniards, as well as by the President and people of the United States." [31]

A month later General Woodford, American Minister to Spain, received his written instructions in which he was informed that it could not "be reasonably asked or expected that a policy of mere inaction can be safely prolonged". In his first meeting with the Spanish Minister for Foreign Affairs, after presenting his credentials in September, Woodford demanded that by November satisfactory assurance be given the United States that early and certain peace could be secured in Cuba.

The reply stated in effect that after Spain had reestablished control of the island, it was her intention to leave to Cuba the control of the island's internal affairs. An indication of a conciliatory policy was the replacement of Weyler by General Ramón Blanco.

The Spanish Government felt some assurance that President McKinley would temporize with the situation at least until after the November elections. In October Dupuy de Lôme had so advised his Government, and added:

[31] Shippee and Way, "William Rufus Day," in *American Secretaries of State*, Vol. IX, p. 47.

"It is indubitable that today he [McKinley] is trying to have the solution of the Cuban question effected in a way that will result in triumph for his personal politics."

At the end of November the Spanish Government promulgated reforms conferring on Cubans all rights of Peninsular Spaniards including the franchise, and outlining a plan of autonomous government. These reforms were known to President McKinley when he drafted his annual message to Congress. Referring to the possibility of intervention, he asked: "Should such a step be now taken when it is apparent that a hopeful change has supervened in the policy of Spain toward Cuba?" [32]

· · · · ·

In the middle of January, 1898, demonstrations and attacks on newspapers advocating autonomy occurred in Havana. The American Consul General, Fitzhugh Lee, telegraphed to the Department of State as follows:

"Uncertainty exists whether Blanco can control the situation. If demonstrated he can not maintain order, preserve life, and keep the peace, or if Americans and their interests are in danger, ships must be sent, and to that end should be prepared to move promptly."

Following this telegram President McKinley determined to send the battleship *Maine* to Havana

[32] James D. Richardson, *op. cit.*, Vol. XIII, p. 6261.

harbor ostensibly as an indication of friendly feeling, and Lee was instructed to "arrange for a friendly interchange of calls with authorities". Dupuy de Lôme protested in vain, but made the best of the situation by arranging for a return visit by a Spanish war vessel.

Then early in February occurred a diplomatic incident that raised the temperature of a public opinion which had been kept at fever heat for months by the rivalry of the *New York Journal* and the *New York World* for sensational Cuban copy. The *Journal* printed a facsimile of a private letter that Dupuy de Lôme had sent to a Spanish Government agent in Cuba, referring to McKinley's annual message of the preceding December as follows:

"Besides the ingrained and inevitable coarseness with which it repeated all that the Press and public opinion in Spain have said about Weyler, it once more shows what McKinley is, weak and a bidder for the admiration of the crowd, besides being a common politician who tries to leave a door open behind himself while keeping on good terms with the jingoes of his party. . . .

"It would be very advantageous to take up, even if only for effect, the question of commercial relations, and to have a man of some prominence sent here in order that I may make use of him to carry on propaganda among the Senators and others in opposition to the junta and try to win over refugees."

Dupuy de Lôme learned of the fate of his letter the day before its publication, and the shrewd diplomat immediately sent in his resignation. This deprived the American Government of some of the satisfaction of a demand for the Minister's dismissal, whose "indiscretion" the Spanish Government "sincerely regretted", and whose words, in accepting his resignation, were "disauthorized". At the same time the Spanish Government maintained that it was committed to "the new Colonial regimen and the projected treaty of commerce".

The U.S.S. *Maine* had arrived in Havana harbor about two weeks before the publication of the Dupuy de Lôme letter and even before our Government could be informed that the Spanish Government had approved of "these demonstrations of cordiality and courtesy to the full extent of their value". During this time there had been no incident to mar the courtesy visit of the *Maine*. However, on the night of February 15th while Captain Sigsbee, in his cabin, was in the act of sealing a letter to his wife in which he remarked "how singularly beautiful" taps sounded "in the oppressive stillness of the night"—his ship was blown up under him.

Two officers and two hundred and sixty-four men of the *Maine* perished in Havana harbor. A naval court of inquiry was immediately appointed and sent to Havana for an investigation. At the end of March it found that:

"... the *Maine* was destroyed by the explosion of a submarine mine, which caused the partial explosion of two or more of the forward magazines.

"The Court has been unable to obtain evidence fixing the responsibility for the destruction of the *Maine* upon any person or persons."

In 1907, on my first visit to Cuba, I saw a weather-beaten turret of the wrecked *Maine* still protruding through the waters of Havana harbor like a gravestone marking the watery sepulcher of those unsuspecting martyrs whose death was to aid the cause of Cuban independence. Four years later the *Maine* was raised, towed out to sea and sunk in deep water with military honors. Before this ceremony a second court of inquiry made a more thorough investigation of the hull of the ship than had been possible before and determined that "a charge of a low form of explosive exterior to the ship" had been detonated at a place on the hull which was not the point where, according to the original board, the explosion had taken place. The destruction of the *Maine* remains an unsolved mystery to this day, which is particularly surprising in a country where fantasy and rumor vie with the tropical burning sun in heat and color, and where there are no secrets among friends.

In the popular mind Spain was responsible for the destruction of the *Maine* no matter how it had occurred; and the popular mind of '98 was steeped in the "martial spirit".

When the news of the sinking of the *Maine* was being shouted by newsboys selling Extras in the streets of New York, I was a small boy of eight. My reaction to the incident is one of the vivid recollections of my boyhood, and indicates how thoroughly the propaganda of the *World* and the *Journal* had roused the American people. When my father heard the news, he hurriedly drove across Central Park to consult with my grandfather, and I for some unknown reason accompanied him. My grandfather lived in a brownstone stoop house with a great bay window that faced the Museum of Natural History. While I gazed through this window across the street to see if I could penetrate the walls of the Museum to glimpse its awe-inspiring animals, my father and grandfather very gravely discussed the possibilities of war with Spain. When the conference ended, my father told me to prepare to go home and solemnly informed me that there might be a war and said: "What do you think of that?" I replied, much to his discomfort, "Hurrah! I'm glad we're going to fight."

While awaiting the naval board's investigation of the cause of the *Maine* disaster, the desire for war grew in Congress and conversely the old proposal for a sale of Cuba by Spain was gaining sympathy in Madrid. The newspaper *El Nacional* said:

"Will nobody preach and proclaim the annexation of Cuba by agreement with Spain on condition that the United States redeem us from the insular debt, favoring us during a certain period by a tariff concession and guaranteeing under a powerful authority and a respected flag the lives and property of Spaniards resident in Cuba?"

However, the sentiment of the American Congress was opposed to involving the United States in any such financial obligation. The Administration apparently had no definite plan for the solution of the Cuban problem and no desire to take the responsibility for one, and therefore preferred drifting. The American Minister requested some definite instructions and wanted consideration given to a purchase, but the only satisfaction that he received from the Department of State was the following telegram of March 20:

". . . Confidential report shows naval board will make unanimous report that *Maine* was blown up by submarine mine. This report must go to Congress soon. Feeling in the United States very acute. . . . *Maine* loss may be peacefully settled if full reparation is promptly made, such as the most civilized nations would offer. But there remains general conditions in Cuba which can not be longer endured, and which will demand action on our part, unless Spain restores honorable peace which will stop starvation of people and give them opportunity to take care of themselves, and restore commerce now wholly lost. April 15 is none too early date for accomplishment of these purposes. Relations will be much influenced by attitude of Spanish Government in *Maine* matter, but general conditions must not be lost sight of. . . ."[33]

[33] U. S. *Foreign Relations, 1898*; Washington, 1901, p. 692.

In turn, Spain was pursuing a policy of vagueness and diplomatic delay apparently in the hope that the foreign powers including the Vatican might mediate in such a way as to save Cuba for Spain, or at least save Spanish prestige. This was indicated by the following communication which the Spanish Minister for Foreign Affairs Gullón sent to his representatives abroad, informing them of his negotiations with Woodford:

> "I shall reply tomorrow that the most elemental justice demands, regarding the *Maine,* a cognizance of the report of the Spanish Commission; its comparison with the American to be done, of course, in a tranquil atmosphere, and outside of Congress; and in the event of irreconcilable disagreement, submission to a decision of other dispassionate judges."

President McKinley sent a message to Congress on April 11th after the Spanish Government had agreed at the eleventh hour to an armistice. In this message he asked Congress "in the name of humanity, in the name of civilization, in behalf of endangered American interests . . . to authorize and empower the President to take measures to secure a full and final termination of hostilities between the Government of Spain and the people of Cuba, and to secure in the island the establishment of a stable government, capable of maintaining order and observing its international obligations, insuring peace and tranquillity and the security of its citizens, as well as our own, and to use the military and naval forces of the United States as may be necessary for these purposes".[34]

A week later Congress passed a Joint Resolution giving the President the powers he asked and ambiguously proclaiming: "That the people of the island of Cuba are and of right ought to be free and independent".

And finally Congress passed the Teller Amendment, that unique profession of international altruism, stating:

"That the United States hereby disclaims any disposition or intention to exercise sovereignty, jurisdiction, or control over said island except for the pacification thereof, and asserts its determination when that is accomplished to leave the government and control of the island to its people".

This formal intervention in Cuba brought a formal declaration of war by Spain and a declaration by the United States Congress of the existence of a state of war.

Thus was brought to an end the first phase of the problem of the relations between the United States and Cuba which had lasted for a century and a quarter and which primarily resulted from the incompetence of Spanish Colonial Government.

American intervention gave to Cuba its independ-

[34] James D. Richardson, *op. cit.*, Vol. XIII, p. 6291.

ence; but it must be remembered that the intervention was itself called into being by long years of persistent struggle on the part of the Cubans themselves. Upon the declaration of war the grand old Cuban philosopher, Enrique José Varona, voiced the sentiments of his countrymen in this tribute to the Cuban martyrs.

"Let our first thoughts be for them: for all those who for generation upon generation during nearly a whole century, did not cease to battle and have died for our liberty; for all those who fell as heroes on the battlefield; for all those who succumbed as martyrs in the glorious cause; for those who died obscurely in filthy underground dungeons; for all those who perished victims to fever in the poisoned woods; for the mute and ghastly victims of the Spanish starvation".[35]

[35] *De la Colonia a la República,* La Habana, 1919, "Discurso," p. 193.

PART II

Formation of Treaty Relationship Between the United States and the Cuban Republic

During the period of the Spanish American War the United States never formally recognized a revolutionary government in Cuba, and its relationship with the Cubans was confined largely to questions connected with military and naval operations. Unfortunately these operations on behalf of the Cuban cause were not greeted with unalloyed enthusiasm; as soon as the Cuban Junta achieved its aim of provoking American intervention, the Cuban attitude toward the intervention suffered a slight change.

Máximo Gómez, Cuba's generalissimo in the field, asked that the Spanish supplies be cut off and that the Cubans be supplied with arms and ammunition and, perhaps, a very much needed force of artillery; but, other than that, he hoped to win the war without the presence of American troops. He wanted the chestnuts pulled out of the fire, but he did not want the Americans to consume them. Perhaps the fear felt by Gómez and other Cuban leaders was not that the Americans would appropriate the chestnuts, but that they might dictate their distribution. The arrival of the American troops, therefore, was not the occasion of the rejoicing which might have been anticipated from the preliminary Cuban propaganda. There was none of that spontaneous acclaim that greeted another American Expeditionary Force when it arrived in France some twenty years later in the World War, and there were few of the warm emotional comradeships that subsequent political bickerings have not effaced from the heart of the American who experienced them. The Cuban, however, unlike the French, was not sure that this American expeditionary force would return home at the end of the war. On the contrary, the actual presence of the American troops aroused suspicion and distrust in Cuba, and this reaction to our friendly intervention throws considerable light on the misunderstanding that has shadowed the natural friendship between the two countries.

Our lack of a well defined foreign policy in Latin America, the inconsistency and, at times, ineptness of our diplomacy there at that period, our apparent hypocrisy in carrying on imperialistic activities in spite of benign official dicta to the contrary—all were firmly fixed in the minds of the Cubans, but had scarcely entered the consciousness of those American troops who came, as they believed, to deliver the Cubans from their oppressors. The American people in general at that period had little interest in and less knowledge of foreign affairs. Only a few Americans with special interests in Latin America followed the news of these countries and of our relations with them. Cubans, on the other hand, were familiar with Latin American history and the part played therein by the United States.

At the same time, the Cuban leaders of the revolution were not the authoritative representatives of a homogeneous people with a well defined public opinion and a well developed political philosophy. The country was divided into many factions with differing interests. At the beginning of the war the different elements in the country included the Spanish political hierarchy which held all governmental posts; the Spanish and a few Cuban and foreign great landlords; the Cuban *guajiro*, or small farmer, who worked the land on shares for his landlord; the black and mulatto Cuban laborer; and the shopkeepers, most of whom were Spanish. Unfortunately, there was no middle class—that all important stabilizing force in the modern state. The absence of a middle class is a heritage from the system of Spanish colonization of Cuba.

In the days of early conquest land was exploited even more crudely than in the pioneering days of our modern capitalistic system. The aborigines of Cuba were enslaved by the conquerors and put to work in the mines and fields of the island until they died of overwork and disease. The resulting scarcity of labor was counteracted by the importation of negro slaves from Africa, whose women mixed their blood freely with that of the Spaniards. A census of the island taken under American supervision during the military occupation indicated a total population of 1,572,797 of which 533,498 or thirty-four per cent. were able to read and write, while sixty-six per cent. were illiterate. About fifty-eight per cent., or considerably more than half the entire population, consisted of native born whites; the foreign whites constituted but nine per cent., and the negro and mixed race about thirty-three per cent.

The Spanish landlords, of course, opposed American intervention. In addition, some of the Cuban and foreign landlords were sympathetic with Spain as they anticipated that their special interests might be better served by a continuation of the Spanish landholding system. Expressions of disfavor toward the first intervention in Cuba were heard almost as soon as the act had taken place, and this has been the fate of succeeding interventions or diplomatic interpositions in Cuban affairs, no matter how urgently they have been solicited.

Despite this reception and the bungling and confusion attendant upon the organization of the expeditionary force, the American troops landed and carried out a successful Cuban campaign. Coöperating with Cuban insurgents, they forced the surrender of the Spanish Army in Cuba on July 17th at the battle of Santiago; while the United States Navy destroyed the Spanish war vessels at Manila and Santiago Bay.

Within ten days after the battle of Santiago Spain asked the United States through the French Government for terms of peace. The terms of peace offered by the United States were accepted with a few verbal changes and incorporated in a protocol which included Spain's "relinquishment" of sovereignty over Cuba, and immediate evacuation of the island. The protocol provided for the appointment of commissioners to meet in Paris not later than October 1st to draw up the definitive treaty of peace.

The treaty negotiations regarding Cuba centered on the disposition to be made of the Cuban debt, which was estimated at from four hundred to six hundred million dollars, and of the meaning and effect of Spain's relinquishment of Cuba. The United States refused to assume or have Cuba burdened with a debt which had largely been contracted for the purpose of Cuba's "pacification" by Spain. Thus it was that *Cuba Libre* started its career in the happy and unusual condition of a country free from the burdens of a national debt.

The Spanish Minister for Foreign Affairs, the Duque de Almodóvar del Río, had stated that Spain was ready to accept "absolute independence, or independence under an American protectorate, or annexation to the United States, preferring annexation because this would guarantee better the security of Spaniards who resided or had estates there." The

Spanish Commissioners at Paris in October endeavored without success to persuade the United States to reconsider its assertion in the Teller Amendment that it would not annex the island. The disposition of Cuba was provided for in the following two articles:

Art. I.

". . . Spain relinquishes all claim of sovereignty over and title to Cuba.

". . . And as the island is, upon its evacuation by Spain, to be occupied by the United States, the United States will, so long as such occupation shall last, assume and discharge the obligations that may under international law result from the fact of its occupation, for the protection of life and property.

Art. XVI.

"It is understood that any obligations assumed in this treaty by the United States with respect to Cuba are limited to the time of its occupancy thereof; but it will, upon the termination of such occupancy, advise any Government established on the island to assume the same obligations." [1]

In spite of the clear provisions of these articles there is a rather widespread misconception in Cuba that the United States is under a perpetual obligation to protect life and property on the island by virtue of the Treaty of Paris. This misconception may be due to the reference to the Treaty in Article III of the Platt Amendment, or it may be merely a popular im-

---

[1] U. S. *Foreign Relations, 1898*; Washington, 1901, pp. 832, 839-840.

FORMING TREATY RELATIONSHIP 53

pression that has been created by those who from time to time have artfully demanded the intervention of the United States on account of "its obligations under the Treaty of Paris."

The island was occupied by the United States under a Military Government reporting to the new Secretary of War, Elihu Root. The latter's appointment indicates the concern with which the United States Government regarded the Cuban situation. As one commentator described it, "Root was called to the telephone to learn that President McKinley wished him to take the Secretaryship of War. Mr. Root replied to the President's secretary that this was 'quite absurd' as he knew 'nothing about war' and 'nothing about the army'. . . . After conferring with the President, the latter's secretary informed Mr. Root that Mr. McKinley 'was not looking for anyone who knows anything about war or for anyone who knows anything about the army'; that he wanted 'a lawyer to direct the government of these Spanish islands' ".[2]

In February 1899 the evacuation of Cuba by the Spanish troops was completed. However, Oriente Province in which is situated the city of Santiago, had been under the administration of Brigadier General Leonard Wood as Commander of the Army of Occupation since the preceding July. On January 1,

---

[2] James Brown Scott, "Elihu Root," in *American Secretaries of State*, Vol. IX, p. 193.

1899 the government of the island was transferred to Major John R. Brooke as Military Governor. His work in bringing the first semblance of order out of chaos was no less difficult than the better known achievements of Brigadier General Leonard Wood who succeeded him at the end of the year.

The difficulties of administering by foreign troops a yellow fever country in the tropics which had been ravaged by a long, cruel, and devasting war were alleviated by the character of the Cuban people. In spite of the relaxing qualities of the tropical sun, the Cuban countryman is a hard and persistent worker whose accomplishments amaze the tyro from a northern land. He is of a far more peace-loving nature than his prototype in other Latin American countries where there has been a strong admixture of Indian blood. The Cuban too has both an extraordinary quickness of mind and wit and a ready adaptability, perhaps developed by his generations of struggle against oppressive rule. His patience in and acceptance of suffering is heroic. He more often than not meets disaster heaped upon misfortune with an appropriate joke and the Spanish proverb:

No hay mal que dure cien años, ni cuerpo que lo resista. (There is no evil that lasts a hundred years nor anybody who withstands it.)

In 1900, at the end of the first year of occupation, Secretary Root summarized the work of the Ameri-

FORMING TREATY RELATIONSHIP 55

can Military Government in Cuba in his report. The policy of the American Administration was to employ Cubans as far as possible, thus training them "in the first steps of systematic self-government." A census was completed, and an election law promulgated. The Administration undertook a complete reorganization of all public works, involving not only the construction of new roads and public buildings, but a complete system of sanitation for the island. Particular attention was given to charitable or social institutions. The hospitals were supplied with medicines and surgical apparatus, and trained nurses were brought from the United States to engage in the instruction of nurses on the island. Secretary Root graphically described the conditions to be corrected, as follows:

"Unless it were in the Mercedes Hospital in Havana, there was not a place in Cuba at the time of American occupation to which a patient could go for either medical or surgical treatment with any reasonable prospect of proper facilities and care.

"The condition of the insane was particularly distressing. They were confined in cells in the jails all over the island, filthy and ragged, and treated literally like wild beasts. All these unfortunates have been collected and taken to the large insane asylum in Havana, which has been put in good order, and they are cared for in accordance with the dictates of modern humanity.

"The prisons in the island were filled to overflowing

with wretched creatures living in indescribable filth and squalor.

"The cruelty of these conditions is more impressive from the fact that many of the unfortunate inmates had never been tried, or convicted of any offense. As the simplest way of dealing with that evil, a board of pardons was constituted in January, which visited all the prisons and examined the inmates. They found many who had been for long periods waiting trial, and in one instance this period had extended for eleven years." [3]

These intolerable delays of criminal procedure were obviated by the establishment of correctional courts throughout the island.

Turning to education, Root pointed out that in December, 1899, the entire public school enrollment on the island numbered 21,435 and that the schools were poorly housed, ridiculously lacking in equipment and, as a result of a fee system, almost entirely closed to the poor. By June, 1900, the enrollment had increased to 143,120. School buildings were renovated, and the old Spanish barracks were made available for educational purposes. Through the generosity of Harvard University and its friends, 1281 Cuban teachers attended a summer school of instruction at Cambridge, designed to fit them for their duty.

Aside from this, the story of the fight against yellow fever is the most interesting episode of the

[3] Elihu Root, *Military and Colonial Policy of the U. S.*, Cambridge, 1916, pp. 200-201.

FORMING TREATY RELATIONSHIP 57

American occupation and certainly its most valuable contribution, not only to Cuba, but to humanity. In announcing to his staff his determination to solve the yellow fever problem, Wood said: "We are going to rid Cuba of yellow fever. But we are going to do even more. We are going to make it certain that at the end of five years there will be practically no yellow fever left anywhere in the world." [4] His prophecy was fulfilled. The American Administration undertook the enormous task of a house-to-house renovation and disinfection in the city of Havana, stamping out the disease there and extending its work throughout the island until yellow fever was completely eradicated from Cuba.

The man who originally surmised the source of yellow fever infection was Dr. Carlos Finlay, a physician of British extraction, born and practising in Cuba. He insisted that the generally accepted culprit, filth, was not the cause, but that mosquitoes were. He had no evidence, but persisted in his theory in spite of the fact that attempts to prove it by subjecting persons to the bites of infected mosquitoes had failed. It was subsequently discovered, as the reason for this, that the yellow fever patient ceases to have the infective agent in his blood after the third day of the disease and so can not infect mosquitoes after that time; and that after the mosquito has bitten a person with yellow fever, even during the first three days, he be-

[4] Hermann Hagedorn, *Leonard Wood*, N. Y., 1931, Vol. I, p. 326.

comes able to infect only after a period of incubation of twelve to fourteen days. These theories were finally demonstrated under a commission composed of Doctors Walter Reed, U.S.A., James Carroll, Ariistides Agramonte and Jesse W. Lazear. The last-named died, a martyr to a noble cause. In addition, Dr. Carroll and a number of gallant soldiers of the United States Army of Occupation voluntarily risked their lives on behalf of humanity in these experiments.[5] A famous physician visiting me at Havana, remarked with feeling: "I see great monuments, parks, and boulevards dedicated to warriors and politicians; there is but a modest bust in a comparatively obscure part of the city in memory of those great benefactors, Finlay, Reed, and his collaborators."

One month after the inauguration of the American Military Government the United States Congress passed a bill known as the Foraker law which prohibited the grant of franchises or concessions during the period of American occupation of Cuba. This measure is evidence of the true attitude of the American people in their relations with Cuba. The official endeavor, which has had few exceptions, has been to prevent the exploitation of Cuba by unscrupulous promoters whether of American or other nationality. Exploitation by foreigners has occasionally taken place in Cuba as it has in other countries of the world.

[5] *Vide* "Roll of Honor" in U. S. *Army Register*, Washington, 1930, pp. 1103-1105.

FORMING TREATY RELATIONSHIP 59

In Cuba it is usually the result of an attempt by dishonest or over-zealous promoters of Cuban and American nationality in combination to enrich themselves at the expense of the country.

. . . . .

The American Military Government has been criticized on the ground that the revised tariff law promulgated by it was "somewhat too distinctly advantageous to American products". Food products were given advantageous tariff schedules which, although temporarily reducing the cost of living, did not encourage a crop diversification for home consumption which might have been of greater benefit to the country eventually.

Secretary Root referring to Cuba's international trade in his report for 1901 stated:

> "Notwithstanding the intimate political relations which have existed between the United States and Cuba since 1898, American production has not succeeded to any considerable degree in superseding the productions of other countries in the Cuban market."

Secretary Root's reports indicate the attempt on the part of the Military Government to bring order out of chaos on the island, and to establish the Republic of Cuba on a sound social, financial, political, and economic basis. The exceptional record of social and cultural achievement should be a refutation of those

North American and Latin American critics and sowers of international discord whose perpetual theme is that materialism is the paramount influence of the United States. The intervention was carried out with an altruism unusual in the dealings of a large and powerful country administering, for a time, a small and weak one. In its trusteeship over Cuba, the United States observed, in the highest sense, those relations that should exist between a ward and a trustee.

Later when the United States entered the World War, Cuba was prompt to recall those relations by issuing its own declaration of war the next day on account of the "obligations more moral than legal that bind us to the United States", as the Cuban Presidential message stated. The United States shortly after made a loan of $15,000,000 to the Cuban Government to enable Cuba to coöperate more effectively. Every dollar of capital and interest was promptly repaid by Cuba.

However, although the Cubans appreciated our assistance in their war for independence and although the American Military Government is acknowledged to have been the most honest and efficient Government that the island has ever had, the Cuban people were quite humanly dissatisfied with a foreign occupation of their country. The echoes of the propaganda to get the Americans into the country had hardly subsided before a new propaganda had started to get

FORMING TREATY RELATIONSHIP 61

them out. The Cubans had suffered patiently and struggled resolutely over a very long period for their freedom; they were impatient to have it consummated.

During his administration, Governor General Wood unearthed a scandal in the finances of the Post Office. Defalcations to the extent of a hundred thousand dollars were traced to the American heads of the Postal Administration. The guilty were promptly tried and convicted, but the incident added fuel to the fire that had been kindled principally by self-seekers to expedite the departure of the Americans. General Wood's biographer, Hermann Hagedorn, cites an illuminating Cuban reaction to the Post Office scandal:

" 'The Spaniards stole everything', remarked the wife of an official whom Wood had deposed, 'and now the Americans are stealing everything. My husband is for independence. Of course, the Cubans will steal, but then the money will stay in the country.' " [6]

In an effort to expedite the American withdrawal from Cuba, Wood issued an order on July 25, 1900, that the Cubans should "elect delegates to a convention . . . to frame and adopt a Constitution for the people of Cuba, and, *as a part thereof,* to provide for and agree with the Government of the United States

[6] Hermann Hagedorn, *op. cit.*, Vol. I, p. 296.

upon the relations to exist between that Government and the government of Cuba . . ." [7]

The phrase italicized was the prologue to the Platt Amendment which has been the issue around which Cuban American relations have revolved ever since. Wood's order was received with dismay by at least the articulate elements in the country. The objectionable phrase was indeed in distinct contrast to Secretary Root's report on Cuba for 1899 which stated: *"When that government is established* the relations which exist between it and the United States will be matter *for free and uncontrolled agreement between the two parties."* [8]

Apparently Secretary Root had had a change of heart or at least a change of mind. In a letter to General Wood on January 9, 1901, he throws some light on the difficulties which the Cuban question imposed:

"I am getting pretty tired of having Congress on the one hand put us under independence of Cuba resolutions, and Foraker franchise resolutions and resolutions of hostile inquiry and criticism, and on the other hand, shirk all responsibility; and I do not relish the prospect of having the Cuban constitution and proposals as to our relations just too late for Congress to act, compelling us to go on and govern for another year, with the Cubans howling at us to do something and the democratic press abusing us because we do not do something, and with the certainty that we will be met

[7] In *Message of the President*, Dec. 3, 1900, H. R. 56th Congress, 2d Sess., Doc. 1, p. XLII.
[8] U. S. War Department Annual Reports, Washington, 1899.

by a denial of our lawful authority if we undertake to do anything and with a possibility of a change for the worse in Cuban conditions."

In the same letter Root hints at the fears of European aggression in Cuba. In reading it we must recall that it was written at a period when there was a good deal of swashbuckling in Europe and especially in Germany; it was many years before the cutting and fortification of the Panama Canal and the development of our modern navy; it was the period when we were emerging from the "second-rate power" class. Secretary Root writes:

"We now have, by virtue of our occupation of Cuba and the terms under which sovereignty was yielded by Spain, a right to protect her which all foreign nations recognize. It is of great importance to Cuba that that right, resting upon the treaty of Paris and derived through that treaty from the sovereignty of Spain, should never be terminated but should be continued by a reservation, with the consent of the Cuban people, at the time when the authority which we now exercise is placed in their hands. If we should simply turn the government over to the Cuban administration, retire from the island, and then turn round to make a treaty with the new government, just as we would make treaties with Venezuela, and Brazil, and England, and France, no foreign State would recognize any longer a right on our part to interfere in any quarrel which she might have with Cuba, unless that interference were based upon an assertion of the Monroe Doctrine. But the Monroe Doctrine is not a part of international law and has never been recognized by European nations. How soon some one of these nations may feel inclined to test the willingness of the United States to make war in support of her assertion of that doctrine, no one can tell. It would be quite unfortunate for Cuba if it should be tested there."

There was much criticism, both temperate and intemperate, of this proposal, which in effect required the Constitutional Assembly to enter into a treaty with the United States. A joint dispatch by the representatives of the political parties in Cuba was sent to President McKinley protesting that the relations between Cuba and the United States were not Constitutional questions and should not form part of the Constitution of Cuba. Under the pressure of protests from both Cuba and the United States assurances were given that the order would be modified. In the election for the Assembly both the nationalist and military groups were successful and together obtained a majority. General Wood called the Assembly together on November 5, 1900, and read to it in part the following:

"It will be your duty, first, to frame and adopt a Constitution for Cuba, and, when that has been done, to formulate what, in your opinion, ought to be the relations between Cuba and the United States.

"The Constitution must be adequate to secure a stable, orderly, and free government.

"When you have formulated the relations which, in your opinion, ought to exist between Cuba and the United States,

FORMING TREATY RELATIONSHIP 65

the Government of the United States will doubtless take such action on its part as shall lead to a final and authoritative agreement between the people of the two countries to the promotion of their common interests.

"All friends of Cuba will follow your deliberations with the deepest interest, earnestly desiring that you shall reach just conclusions, and, that by the dignity, individual self-restraint, and wise conservatism which shall characterize your proceedings, the capacity of the Cuban people for representative government may be signally illustrated.

"The fundamental distinction between true representative government and dictatorship is that in the former every representative of the people, in whatever office, confines himself strictly within the limits of his defined powers. Without such restraint there can be no free constitutional government.

"Under the order pursuant to which you have been elected and convened, you have no duty and no authority to take part in the present government of the Island. Your powers are strictly limited by the terms of that order." [9]

Wood then verbally explained that "they had been elected to frame a Constitution for Cuba. That was their plain duty. The matter of relations which should exist between Cuba and the United States was another matter."

The Convention was satisfied and telegraphed to President McKinley "its sentiment of thanks to the American people."

General Wood officially left the Assembly to its own resources although in a letter to Secretary Root

[9] Albert G. Robinson, *Cuba and the Intervention*, N. Y., 1905, pp. 211-212.

in the previous spring he had said he was "going to work on a Constitution for the Island similar to our own".

In studying the history of the Republic and living through a turbulent part of it, one cannot fail to put the question whether one of the faults of the Cuban Constitution is not its too great similarity to our own. A Constitution framed as was ours for a union of widespread independent States with some experience in self-government and with the Anglo-Saxon traditions of majority rule and a respect for individual rights might not fit a one-crop island country composed of heterogeneous social elements which for hundreds of years had been under the heel of autocratic government. In fact, the looseness of fit of Cuba's Constitutional harness has perhaps been an incentive to slip it off when the rubbing became irksome.

Rafael Martínez Ortiz, Cuban historian of the period, and a diplomat and statesman who in his old age was the Secretary of State in office upon my arrival in Cuba, comments on the framing of the Constitution: "The North American influence had been universally felt; the apparent simplicity of the representative system satisfied the needs and the desires; there appeared before their eyes the perfect governmental formula."

Martínez Ortiz goes on to point out that the ex-

FORMING TREATY RELATIONSHIP 67

ample of the United States had always appealed to Latin America. He says:

> "The division of the powers, following the beautiful theoretical conception of Montesquieu, revolving with relative independence and with a coördinated and synchronized movement, had found such a brilliant and appealing practical solution in the great Republic that it tempted the statesmen and induced them to apply to their respective countries the same representative system." [10]

What has, perhaps, been overlooked by Latin America is that these powers only revolved "with relative independence and with a coördinated and synchronized movement", under the pressure of an enlightened public opinion supporting such stalwart champions of the "division of the powers" as John Marshall and his successors.

While the Constitutional Assembly was undertaking its important work, Root was apparently much concerned with the responsibility involved in terminating the military occupation of Cuba. On February 9, 1901, he made a masterly presentation of the Administration's thesis on the relationship that should exist between Cuba and the United States. It is of such importance that I quote at length from his letter to General Wood. He states that during the occupation provided for by the Treaty of Paris:

[10] *Los Primeros Años de Independencia,* Paris, Vol. I, pp. 191-193.

"we were to discharge international obligations, protect the rights of the former subjects of Spain, and cause or permit the establishment of a government to which we could, in good faith, commit the protection of the lives and property and personal rights of those inhabitants from whom we had compelled their former sovereign to withdraw her protection. It is plain that the government to which we were thus to transfer our temporary obligations should be a government based upon the peaceful suffrages of the people of Cuba, representing the entire people and holding their power from the people, and subject to the limitations and safeguards which the experience of constitutional government has shown to be necessary to the preservation of individual rights. This is plain as a duty to the people of Cuba under the resolution of April 20, 1898, and it is plain as an obligation of good faith under the Treaty of Paris. Such a government we have been persistently and with all practicable speed building up in Cuba, and we hope to see it established and assume control under the provisions which shall be adopted by the present convention. It seems to me that no one familiar with the traditional and established policy of this country in respect to Cuba can find cause for doubt as to our remaining duty. It would be hard to find any single statement of public policy which has been so often officially declared by so great an array of distinguished Americans authorized to speak for the Government of the United States, as the proposition stated, in varying but always uncompromising and unmistakable terms, that the United States would not under any circumstances permit any foreign power other than Spain to acquire possession of the Island of Cuba.

"Jefferson and Monroe and John Quincy Adams and Jackson and Van Buren and Grant and Clay and Webster and Buchanan and Everett have all agreed in regarding this as essential to the interests and the protection of the United States. The United States has, and will always have, the most vital interest in the preservation of the independence which she has secured for Cuba, and in preserving the people of that island from the domination and control of any foreign power whatever. The preservation of that independence by a country so small as Cuba, so incapable, as she must always be, to contend by force against the great powers of the world, must depend upon her strict performance of international obligations, upon her giving due protection to the lives and property of the citizens of all other countries within her borders, and upon her never contracting any public debt which in the hands of the citizens of foreign powers shall constitute an obligation she is unable to meet. The United States has, therefore, not merely a moral obligation arising from her destruction of Spanish authority in Cuba and the obligations of the Treaty of Paris for the establishment of a stable and adequate government in Cuba, but it has a substantial interest in the maintenance of such a government.

"We are placed in a position where, for our own protection, we have by reason of expelling Spain from Cuba, become the guarantors of Cuban independence and the guarantors of a stable and orderly government protecting life and property in that island. Fortunately the condition which we deem essential for our own interests is the condition for which Cuba has been struggling, and which the duty we have assumed toward Cuba on Cuban grounds and for Cuban interests requires. It would be a most lame and impotent conclusion if, after all the expenditure of blood and treasure by the people of the United States for the freedom of Cuba and by the people of Cuba for the same object, we should, through the constitution of the new government, by inadvertence or otherwise, be placed in a worse condition in regard to our own vital interests than we were while Spain was in possession, and the people of Cuba should be deprived of that protection and aid from the United States which is necessary to the maintenance of their independence. . . .

"And it was with a view to the proper settlement and disposition of these necessary relations that the order for the election of delegates to the present constitutional convention provided that they should frame and adopt a constitution for the people of Cuba, and as a part thereof provide for and agree with the Government of the United States upon the relations to exist between that Government and the Government of Cuba.

"The people of Cuba should desire to have incorporated in her fundamental law, provisions in substance as follows:

" '1. That no government organized under the constitution shall be deemed to have authority to enter into any treaty or engagement with any foreign power which may tend to impair or interfere with the independence of Cuba, or to confer upon such foreign power any special right or privilege without the consent of the United States.

" '2. That no government organized under the constitution shall have authority to assume or contract any public debt in excess of the capacity of the ordinary revenues of the island after defraying the current expenses of government, to pay the interest.

" '3. That upon the transfer of the control of Cuba to the government established under the new constitution, Cuba consents that the United States reserve and retain the right of intervention for the preservation of Cuban independence and the maintenance of a stable government, adequately protecting life, property, and individual liberty, and discharging the obligations with respect to Cuba imposed by the Treaty of Paris on the United States and now assumed and undertaken by the Government of Cuba.

FORMING TREATY RELATIONSHIP 71

" '4. That all the acts of the Military Government, and all rights acquired thereunder, shall be valid and shall be maintained and protected.

" '5. That to facilitate the United States in the performance of such duties as may devolve upon her under the foregoing provisions and for her own defense, the United States may acquire and hold the title to land for naval stations, and maintain the same at certain specified points.' " [11]

This letter was communicated to the Committee on Relations from the Cuban Constitutional Assembly on February 15th. Up to this time Martínez Ortiz says "the Assemblymen had been running on a path of roses". Four days before, debate had ended on the articles of the Constitution, which the members of the Convention signed on the 21st of February. The effect of the Root document on the assembly is described by Martínez Ortiz as follows:

"General Wood's declarations excited the members of the Assembly. The reality was far graver than they had anticipated it would be. The actual disenchantment suffered appeared in their eyes of greater magnitude than they admitted. The Committee met in private session, but the state of animus was reflected at least in part by the newspapers. Only one hope remained: the opinion of Mr. McKinley and of his Secretary Root might not be that of Congress." [12]

Evidently relying on that hope, the Assembly, in a public session on February 27th, approved a report of the Committee on Relations, which follows in part:

[11] Elihu Root, *op. cit.*, pp. 209-212.
[12] Rafael Martínez Ortiz, *op. cit.*, Vol. I, p. 272.

"... We are the delegates of the people of Cuba. Therefore our primary duty lies in interpreting the will and serving the necessities of our people. It was apparent that the intimations of the American Executive contained only the expression of what, in *his* judgment, the people of Cuba ought to desire in the matter of future relations ... It is clear and plain that this is sufficient reason for our giving them [the opinions of the American Executive] a careful consideration.... But we have a complete right to accept or reject them, to select from them that which we think fit, to add to them or to subtract from them, or to substitute for them others according to the dictates of our consciences, holding always before us our duty to reconcile all that may be a legitimate interest or a rational proposal of the people of the United States, with our own highest interests and sacred rights.

"The undersigned committee, while accepting the starting point of the American Executive—which provides that the independence of Cuba shall remain absolutely guaranteed—is of the opinion that some of these stipulations are not acceptable, inasmuch as they modify the independence and sovereignty of Cuba. Our duty consists in making Cuba independent of all other nations, including the great and noble American nation; and if we bind ourselves to ask the consent of the United States to our international treaties; if we allow them to retain the right to intervene in our country to support or displace administrations, and to fulfil rights which only concern the Cuban Government; and if, lastly, we concede to them the right to acquire and maintain any title over any lands whereon they may establish naval stations, it is plain that we should appear to be independent of the rest of the world, but surely we should never be so with relation to the United States." [13]

[13] Albert G. Robinson, *op. cit.*, p. 238.

FORMING TREATY RELATIONSHIP

After this and a further expression of views the report stated that the Convention was of the opinion that if the "Constitutional Powers of the Republic of Cuba saw fit, they might declare:

"1. The Government of the Republic of Cuba shall not enter into any treaty or agreement with any foreign Power or Powers which might compromise or limit the independence of Cuba, or which might, in any way, authorize any foreign Power or Powers to acquire, through colonization or for military or naval purposes, any lodgment, authority or right over any portion of Cuba.

"2. The Government of the Republic of Cuba will not permit its territory to be used as a base of war operations against the United States or any other nation.

"3. The Government of the Republic of Cuba accepts in its entirety the Treaty of Paris of the 10th of December, 1898, in that which it affirms of the rights of the Cubans as well as the obligations which are tacitly imposed, and especially as concerns the obligations imposed by international law, referring to the protection of life and property, accepting for itself the obligations assumed by the United States in this regard, according to Articles I and XVI of said Treaty of Paris.

"4. The Government of the Republic of Cuba shall recognize as legally valid the acts executed by the Military Government, during the term of its occupation, for the good government of Cuba, as well as the rights acquired under said acts, and in conformity with the Joint Resolution, and the second section of the United States Army Bill of 1899–1900, known as the Foraker Bill, and with the existing laws in force in the country.

"5. The Government of the United States and that of

74 THE UNITED STATES AND CUBA

the Republic of Cuba shall regulate their commercial relations by means of a treaty based on reciprocity with a tendency toward the free interchange of their natural and manufactured products, and which will mutually assure them ample special advantages in their respective markets." [14]

In the meanwhile from the United States Government's viewpoint, according to Root, "everything here is getting into beautiful shape", and the shape finally assumed was the now famous Platt Amendment, a document unique in the history of nations. On February 25th the Senate Committee on Cuba reported favorably to the Senate an amendment to the Army Appropriation Bill introduced by Senator Platt, providing:

"That in fulfillment of the declaration contained in the joint resolution approved April 20, 1898, entitled 'For the recognition of the independence of the people of Cuba demanding that the Government of Spain relinquish its authority and government in the island of Cuba, and to withdraw its land and naval forces from Cuba and Cuban waters, and directing the President of the United States to use the land and naval forces of the United States to carry these resolutions into effect,' the President is hereby authorized to 'leave the government and control of the island of Cuba to its people' so soon as a government shall have been established in said island under a constitution which, either

[14] *Ibid.*, pp. 239-240.

FORMING TREATY RELATIONSHIP

as a part thereof or in an ordinance appended thereto, shall define the future relations of the United States with Cuba, substantially as follows:

I.

"That the government of Cuba shall never enter into any treaty or other compact with any foreign power or powers which will impair or tend to impair the independence of Cuba, nor in any manner authorize or permit any foreign power or powers to obtain by colonization or for military or naval purposes or otherwise lodgment in or control over any portion of said island.

II.

"That said government shall not assume or contract any public debt to pay the interest upon which and to make reasonable sinking-fund provision for the ultimate discharge of which the ordinary revenues of the island, after defraying the current expenses of government, shall be inadequate.

III.

"That the government of Cuba consents that the United States may exercise the right to intervene for the preservation of Cuban independence, the maintenance of a government adequate for the protection of life, property, and individual liberty, and for discharging the obligations with respect to Cuba imposed by the treaty of Paris on the United States, now to be assumed and undertaken by the government of Cuba.

IV.

"That all acts of the United States in Cuba during its military occupancy thereof are ratified and validated, and all lawful rights acquired thereunder shall be maintained and protected.

V.

"That the government of Cuba will execute, and as far as necessary, extend the plans already devised or other plans to be mutually agreed upon, for the sanitation of the cities of the island, to the end that a recurrence of epidemic and infectious diseases may be prevented, thereby assuring protection to the people and commerce of Cuba, as well as to the commerce of the southern ports of the United States and the people residing therein.

VI.

"That the Isle of Pines shall be omitted from the proposed constitutional boundaries of Cuba, the title thereto being left to future adjustment by treaty.

VII.

"That to enable the United States to maintain the independence of Cuba, and to protect the people thereof, as well as for its own defense, the government of Cuba will sell or lease to the United States lands necessary for coaling or naval stations at certain specified points, to be agreed upon with the President of the United States.

VIII.

"That by way of further assurance the government of Cuba will embody the foregoing provisions in a permanent treaty with the United States." [15]

The Platt Amendment was presented on behalf of the Administration. It was based upon Root's letter

---

[15] *Congressional Record*, 56th Congress, 2d Sess., p. 2954. *Idem*, p. 3145.

of February 9th which he had read to the Cabinet and then left with the President. Some changes were made in it by him, after which it was given to Senator Platt who drew the Amendment with three new articles. Article V assured a continuance of the Wood sanitation program. The inclusion of this provision had been suggested by General Wood in a letter to Secretary Root. Article VI temporarily excluded the Isle of Pines from the boundaries of Cuba, apparently because of Senator Platt's desire to retain the island as "the most advantageous point from which to defend the entrance to the Isthmian Canal". Similarly Gonzalo de Quesada, who was a member of the Cuban Constitutional Assembly and later the first Minister to Washington, stated "that the Isle of Pines could be made the basis of defense for American interests in the Caribbean Sea, or that, if the Isle of Pines was found unsuitable—as it was afterwards shown to be—for coaling and naval purposes, it could be made the basis of negotiations for the acquisition of other sites."

American land promoters supplemented this effort to retain the Isle of Pines by bringing political pressure to bear upon Congress to keep the island, basing their claim on Article II of the Treaty of Paris which "cedes to the United States the island of Porto Rico and other islands now under Spanish sovereignty in the West Indies". They contended that the Isle of Pines was not a part of Cuba, but one of the "other islands". In 1903 Secretary Root wrote to Senator Platt: "I think at the time the treaty was made it was as much a part of Cuba as Nantucket is a part of Massachusetts".

These factors prevented the ratification of any agreement assigning the island to Cuba; and this injustice was not rectified until 1925, when, under the able negotiations of the talented Cuban Ambassador to Washington, Cosme de la Torriente, "the future adjustment of the Isle of Pines" was then made in favor of Cuba, and the island became part of the Cuban nation, which nature intended it to be.

But this diplomatic skirmish over the Isle of Pines took its toll in casualties among the innocent American bystanders who had gone there, led on by land promoters who originally proclaimed American ownership of the island. Citrus fruit groves and truck farms were established in the false hope that their products raised under the benign stimulus of this fecund land would also be under the benign protection of the American tariff. When visiting the Isle of Pines, I first flew over the entire island to inspect these once extensive and well cultivated groves. Afterwards I visited with the remaining members of the original American colony who were disenchanted by what seemed to them an unwarranted sacrifice of the island, discouraged by ever-increasing tariff rates against their products, impoverished by the world depression, but nevertheless making a valiant fight in

FORMING TREATY RELATIONSHIP 79

the best American spirit to preserve their farms, still hopeful that a saner world economic order would one day mitigate their heavy tariff burdens.

The final addition by Senator Platt was Article VIII which assured the permanence of these Constitutional provisions by their incorporation in a permanent treaty with the United States.

In addition to these new articles there were two important changes in Article III which distinguished Senator Platt's amendment from Secretary Root's original project. These changes, the second one of which became particularly important during the Machado régime, were as follows:

Root had stipulated that the Cuban Government consent that the United States *"reserve and retain* the right of intervention"; Senator Platt provided that the Cuban Government consent that the United States *"may exercise the right to intervene."* Root considered it preferable to affirm the right as already existing and therefore calling merely for retention, but did not believe the matter of sufficient importance to ask Platt to alter his phrasing. In the second place, Root's original draft speaks of the right to intervene for the "maintenance of a stable government *adequately protecting* life, property and individual liberty." Platt spoke of a government *"adequate for* the protection" etc. Root admits a great difference between these phrases; had his original language been retained, the interpretation so often urged—that the United States may intervene whenever the Cuban Government fails in any given case to protect life, liberty or property—would have a reasonable foundation. But under the language actually used, as Root later made clear, intervention seems to be permissible only when the Cuban Government is not one which is adequate for giving such protection, whether or not it actually does give it in particular instances.

The Platt Amendment, thus modified from Wood's original presentation to the Cuban Constitutional Assembly, went to the Senate and the House for debate. The *Congressional Record* of the period is replete with moderate and immoderate oratory on the subject. It is of interest to hear again at least some of the more moderate voices of the representatives of the American people in typical debate on the Cuban question:

> Senator Hoar: Mr. President, I wish to say in a single sentence that, studying this amendment as well as I can, it seems to me eminently wise and satisfactory. I am not able to share in the apprehensions or objections which some Senators in the Chamber have expressed. It seems to me to be, in substance, a proper and necessary stipulation for the application of the Monroe Doctrine to the nearest outlying country in America, except Mexico, whose borders touch our own, and under the circumstances one which the protection of the United States as well as the protection of Cuba fairly and properly requires. (*Cong. Record*, Vol. 34, Part 4, p. 3145)

FORMING TREATY RELATIONSHIP

Senator Morgan: I should like to have the opportunity of merely stating my position; that is all. I do not want to filibuster here, but there will be filibustering going on between this country and Cuba if you adopt that, as that is a nest of filibustering.

It is an invitation to it. And when they want to go down there to rectify the Cubans we will keep a sort of Sunday school down there with an army, at any time and every time that they do not do exactly what we want them to do. They will never put themselves into that attitude. We could not extend a better invitation to those high-tempered and honorable people to rebel, to kick at least against what we are doing, than to put in that provision, which is continuous.

The Senator from South Carolina asked me when it would end. I will tell him never, in my opinion. It is continuous, giving us a right to interfere with their method of conducting their own government in respect to their own people, and then trying to house that or shelter it under the idea of the Monroe Doctrine.

Whoever heard of such an application as that made of the Monroe Doctrine before, that it gives us the right not only to fence off outside the United States and prevent them from coming in and establishing institutions that might be dangerous to the liberties of the United States, sooner or later, but also the right to enter into these different governments, to visit them, look into their affairs, to determine whether or not their governments are adequate to the protection of the life, personal liberty, and property of their own people? (*Ibid.*, p. 3148)

Representative Corliss: . . . I hope and expect that the adoption of the present amendment may continue our sovereignty and induce the people of Cuba to voluntarily ask for the annexation of Cuba, and thereby extend the blessings of humanity for which our country intervened. (*Ibid.*, p. 3341)

Representative Sparkman: . . . But that was not all this remarkable document, which will ever live in history as the grandest triumph of our Christian civilization or the blackest exhibition of national perfidy the world has ever seen, contained; for it further declared that the United States had no disposition or intention to exercise sovereignty, jurisdiction, or control over said island except for the pacification thereof, and asserted the determination of the American government that when this should have been accomplished to leave the government and control of the island of Cuba to its people. (*Ibid.*, p. 3344)

Representative Littlefield: . . . It is not a very long step from the right to intervene to the obligation to exercise that right when its exercise is demanded by those in whose interests it may be assumed the right was conceded. No one can tell under what circumstances it might be insisted by foreign capital, to illustrate, that the Cuban government was inadequate to protect property and individual liberty, or when it might be asserted by a foreign government in the interests of the personal or property rights of its citizens residing therein or having relations therewith that the government was inadequate, and we must protect them in that regard . . .

In section seven the purpose for which the coaling or naval stations are to be acquired is stated as follows: "To enable the United States to maintain the independence of Cuba and to protect the people thereof, as well as for its own defense." When we acquire and occupy territory "to protect the people thereof" it is not a strained construction to hold that we are by virtue thereof bound "to protect the people thereof".

FORMING TREATY RELATIONSHIP 83

This is the principal purpose of any government that may be established "by the inhabitants of Cuba".

Against whom are we "to protect the people thereof", and what occasion is there for protecting "the people thereof" if we maintain, as we insist we wish to do under section three, a "government adequate for the protection of life, property, and individual liberty"? What legitimate occasion have we to "protect the people thereof" when there is or ought to be in existence a "free, independent government established by its people" for that very purpose? Are we to protect them against internal disorder, against their own government, or against foreign governments? Evidently the rights to be conceded by section three were not sufficiently broad and comprehensive, and in order to make our control more absolute and complete this extremely general language was added in section seven. (*Ibid.*, p. 3381)

There was some protest against the irregularity of railroading through as a rider to the Army Appropriation Bill a measure so important to the relations between Cuba and the United States. The opposition in the Senate promptly proposed an amendment to the Amendment striking out the words "The maintenance of a government adequate for the protection of life, property and individual liberty". This was defeated by a vote of 43 to 21. Senator Platt at one stage during the parliamentary fencing, in refusing to withdraw the Amendment, made a prophecy: "I think it is very important that it should be passed at this session and upon this bill. *I believe it will settle* what may be called the Cuban question satisfactorily to the people of Cuba and satisfactorily to our own people".

The Senate adopted the bill on February 27th by a vote of 43 to 20. The House signified its concurrence on March 1st by a vote of 161 to 137. Insofar as the United States Government was concerned, the status of the future relations with Cuba was determined.

. . . . .

In Cuba, the lingering and last hope that "the opinion of Mr. McKinley and of his Secretary Root might not be that of Congress" was lost. The Constitutional Assembly received the news with consternation. The newspaper *La Patria*, the organ of the majority party in the Assembly, stated:

> "The action of the United States respecting Cuba continues to be the theme of conversation in all circles, and there is no occasion to hide the fact that a great majority have received it with displeasure and judge it harshly."

During the first flush of disappointment two resolutions were proposed in the Assembly, recommending to the consideration of the future Government of Cuba clauses 1, 2, 4 and 5; but that clauses 3, 6, and 7 of said Amendment "were considered as impairing the independence and sovereignty of the Island of Cuba and contrary to the letter and spirit of the Joint Resolution of April 19, 1898, on account of which an

FORMING TREATY RELATIONSHIP 85

identical recommendation regarding these clauses could not be made".

The President of the Convention, Dr. Méndez Capote, counseled calm and prudence, and reaffirmed the desire of all Cubans "to maintain bonds of friendship and affection with the people of North America".

Martínez Ortiz states that in the provinces there gradually formed an opinion favorable to the acceptance of the Amendment; that the educated population especially understood the "natural development of and the significance of the problem"; and that the assurance that the military government must be borne indefinitely if the Platt Amendment was not accepted "changed intolerance to resignation".

However, in Havana there was no disposition by the politicians to give up the struggle against the Amendment. The cartoons of the period, an important feature of Cuban life, were surpassing even their customary vigor. On Good Friday *La Discusión* published a cartoon, "The Cuban Calvary". Upon the central cross there hung a figure representing Cuba; upon the crosses on either side, General Wood appeared as Dimas, and President McKinley as Gestas. In the foreground the agonized Mary was represented as public opinion. Senator Platt in the guise of the Roman soldier Longinus presented on a spearhead a sponge marked "Platt Amendment". Wood suspended the publication of the paper for a day. He wrote his friend Theodore Roosevelt regarding the politicians:

> "They see that the sentiment of the country is gradually swinging against them, and their purpose is to provoke me into some action which would make martyrs of them. Heaven pity any man who has to take charge of a situation like this in times of reconstruction. He will require all his own patience, and all he can borrow, to tide him over." [16]

Wood did not lack the required patience in dealing with the members of the Constitutional Convention, but firmly passed on his instructions that "the Platt Amendment is of course final and the members of the Convention who may be responsible for refusing to establish relations on that basis will only injure themselves and their country". He suggested that the Cubans be reassured on certain parts of the Platt Amendment, to which Root replied on March 29th:

> "I hope you have been able to disabuse the minds of members of the Convention of the idea that the intervention described in the Platt amendment is synonymous with intermeddling or interference with the affairs of a Cuban government. It of course means only the formal action of the Government of the United States, based upon just grounds of actual failure or imminent danger, and is in fact but a declaration or acknowledgment of the right to do what the United States did in April, 1898, as the result of the failure of Spain to govern Cuba. It gives to the United States no right which she does not already possess and which she

[16] Hermann Hagedorn, *op. cit.*, Vol. I, p. 363.

FORMING TREATY RELATIONSHIP

would not exercise, but it gives her, for the benefit of Cuba, a standing as between herself and foreign nations in the exercise of that right which may be of immense value in enabling the United States to protect the independence of Cuba." [17]

To this General Wood replied as follows:

"Conference today many leading members Convention believe everything will go through if I can assure them officially that the President and your views of the interpretation and scope of the third clause of the Platt amendment are as stated in your personal letter of March 29th. They believe that this will put it in such shape that it can be accepted by the Convention. It is most important to do this if possible, for the radical members are using the argument that under the third clause, we can intervene for trifling reasons. An official assurance that intervention will be only under conditions such as stated in your letter of March 29th will remove this impression and destroy this argument."

Root's answer on April 2nd established, with the subsequent addition of one word, the official interpretation of the Platt Amendment.

"You are authorized to state officially that in the view of the President the intervention described in the third clause of the Platt amendment is not synonymous with intermeddling or interference with the affairs of the Cuban Government, but the formal action of the Government of the United States, based upon just and substantial grounds, for the preservation of Cuban independence and the main-

[17] *Ibid.*, Vol. I, p. 362.

tenance of a government adequate for the protection of life, property and individual liberty and for discharging the obligations with respect to Cuba imposed by the Treaty of Paris on the United States."

On April 3rd, Wood cabled that the last part of Root's telegram of the preceding day had caused some misunderstanding and asked whether it could not be made to read as follows: "Adequate for protection of life and property and adequate for discharging the obligations with respect to Cuba imposed by the Treaty of Paris on the United States". It will be noted that this suggested change omits reference to the protection of "individual liberty". It was also designed to indicate that it was the Cuban Government which must be adequate to fulfill the obligations of the Treaty of Paris and that it was not the intention of the United States to intervene directly to carry out those obligations. This second aspect was accepted by Root but, in his telegram of April 3rd, he retained the phrase regarding individual liberty, so that the concluding words finally read: ". . . the maintenance of a government adequate for the protection of life and property and individual liberty, and adequate for discharging the obligations with respect to Cuba imposed by the Treaty of Paris on the United States".

This interpretation seems to have been received with great satisfaction by the Cubans, but opposition did not entirely cease. On April 15th, Wood cabled that a Committee would be appointed to proceed to Wash-

FORMING TREATY RELATIONSHIP 89

ington to discuss the Platt Amendment. The General reported that the object really was to accept it, but that this must not under any circumstances become known. He earnestly advised in favor of the Committee's visit. On the same day, Secretary Root replied that the President would be pleased to receive such a Committee.

The Committee, headed by Méndez Capote, President of the Constitutional Convention, arrived in Washington on April 24, 1901, and was courteously welcomed. The members were received by the President and then referred to the Secretary of War for detailed discussion of their business. Several long conferences took place. There were no authorized transcripts of the conversations, but the members of the Committee appear to have taken elaborate notes. Their version of the conference was submitted to the Convention on their return, but was not published until 1918 when it appeared in a volume of *Memoria* of the Cuban Senate, covering the years 1902–1904.

The report in question has since been much quoted both in Cuba and the United States and is undoubtedly relied upon by many Cubans as the authentic interpretation of the Platt Amendment which was taken by the Constitutional Convention as the basis for its acceptance. It seems that the reports of Root's statements are fairly accurate since they coincide closely with the views he expressed in correspondence with Wood. On April 25th the Committee members met with the Secretary of War and explained the doubts and difficulties with which they were faced. Root stated that he would be glad to discuss these matters with them after they had been presented to the President, and this presentation occurred immediately. That afternoon and the next day the Committee spent many hours with Secretary Root going over in detail all the provisions of the Platt Amendment.

According to the Committee's report, Root began with an analysis of the traditional policy of the United States toward Cuba. His stress throughout was upon the need for conserving Cuban independence. He stated that the spirit and aim of the Platt Amendment were to establish Cuba as a sovereign and independent nation and that going beyond that, the United States wished to guarantee Cuba's stability as a free and independent nation. The President of the Committee said he thought it might be difficult for the new Cuban Government to obtain the recognition of other nations in view of the terms of the Platt Amendment, but Root replied that the other nations would follow the United States in recognizing the independence of Cuba.

In regard to the naval bases, Root said they would never be used as points of observation of the internal Government of Cuba; that they were desired solely in the mutual interests of both countries to assure protection from foreign attack.

The President of the Committee tried to obtain

FORMING TREATY RELATIONSHIP

the formal promise of the United States Executive for economic measures favorable to Cuban products, and attempted also to find out the American opinion on the subject. Speaking for himself and in the name of the President, Root gave assurance that if the Cuban Government, when established, appointed representatives to discuss commercial relations, the President would immediately appoint his representatives to negotiate a treaty on the basis of mutual benefits and friendly relations.

On the following day Root handed them a copy of a letter from Senator Platt with which, he stated, he and the President were in complete accord. The letter read as follows:

"I am in receipt of your letter of this date [April 26], in which you say that the members of the Commission of the Cuban Constitutional Convention fear that the provisions relative to intervention, made in the third clause of the Amendment which has come to bear my name, may have the effect of preventing the independence of Cuba, and in reality establish a protectorate or suzerainty by the United States; and you request that I express my views on the questions raised. In reply I beg to state that the Amendment was carefully prepared with the object of avoiding any possible idea that by the acceptance thereof the Constitutional Convention will thereby establish a protectorate or suzerainty, or in any manner whatsoever compromise the independence or sovereignty of Cuba; and speaking for myself, it seems impossible that any such construction can be placed upon that clause. I think the Amendment must be considered as a whole, and it must be evident that its well defined purpose is to secure and safeguard Cuban independence and to establish at the outset a definite understanding of the friendly disposition of the United States towards the Cuban people, and the expressed intention to assist them, if necessary, in the maintenance of such independence. These are my views, and though, as you suggest, I cannot speak for the whole Congress, my belief is that such purpose was well understood by that body."

The Cuban report states:

"Mr. Méndez Capote says: According to what the Secretary has said, it is to be understood that there will be no interference in the Cuban Government, which will enjoy absolute independence. Precisely, answers the Secretary. Mr. Méndez Capote sums up the assertions of the Secretary according to which intervention will be possible only in case of a foreign threat, either against the Cuban Government, or in combination or alliance with the Cubans, or in case of the absence of any Government in Cuba. Precisely, answers the Secretary. To other suggestions of the President of the Committee the Secretary replies: that intervention will never be against the absolute independence of Cuba, that never will there be military interference in the Island in the nature of occupation; that all the bases of the Platt Amendment that speak of interference have for their only object the maintenance of the independence of Cuba; that the Platt Amendment limits distinctly the rights which the American Government believes it has regarding intervention in Cuba and that intervention can only take place in defense of the independence of Cuba and whenever such independence is actually menaced.

"The President of the Committee questions why the

United States, if it believes that it has the right to intervene, and has the power to carry out such intervention, asks the consent of the Cubans. The Secretary replies that the expression of this consent facilitates for the United States the carrying out of its well known intentions regarding other nations.

"Mr. Méndez Capote alleges that this consent would be worth nothing if the United States were not strong enough to carry out its purpose, since strength is the 'ultima ratio' in international questions. The Secretary replies that this is not entirely true. That if force is the deciding factor, it is also true that it does not always shape and inspire international law, for if the legality of certain laws were not respected nations like Switzerland, Belgium and Holland would already have ceased to exist. Certain laws must therefore be enforced, which is the only source of strength of the little nations, in order that the greater nations may not appear as enemies of mankind. A small State intrenched behind laws recognized by all commands as much strength as all the large Nations. And the United States, in addition to the strength on which it relies, seeks the added power of the law to interpose, with strength and with authority, in any attack against the independence of Cuba. The United States proposes to draw up with Cuba a treaty which of itself has a tendency to obviate the necessity of intervening in favor of the independence of Cuba, but it does not want such intervention, if the situation makes intervention necessary, to be disputed by anybody."

There is only a brief discussion of Article II which is coupled with that on Article I and reads as follows:

"To suggestion of the President of the Committee relative to clauses 1 and 2 of the Amendment, the Secretary replied that they treat of strictly internal constitutional limits, which was requested of the Cubans by the American Congress in accordance with the methods of the Constitution of the United States in limiting the power of Congress and placing beyond it certain authority which might endanger the independence of the nation; that the limitations that it asks of us are of the same constitutional character as those which the American Constitution decrees; that they refer to Cuba only and that they will be exercised by Cuba and by the Cubans exclusively."

An explanation was asked by a member of the Committee regarding the sanitary projects referred to in Article V. The Secretary stated that definite plans did not exist and that the article referred to the plans that might be mutually determined by the American and Cuban Governments.

The Committee returned to Cuba and reported to the Convention. On May 17 General Wood cabled Secretary Root that Méndez Capote informed him the Platt Amendment would be accepted, but that they would insert two paragraphs of explanation, in conformity with the statements made by Root to their Committee. On the third article, the following was proposed:

"Third. The Government of the Republic of Cuba consents that the United States by formal action may exercise the right to intervene for the preservation of Cuban independence whenever threatened from without, or, when a state of anarchy exists in the Island to reëstablish in accordance with the constitution of the Republic of Cuba a Gov-

FORMING TREATY RELATIONSHIP 95

ernment adequate for the protection of life, property and individual liberty and to fulfill the obligations imposed by the Treaty of Paris with respect to Cuba."

On the seventh article, the following:

"Seventh. In order to place the United States in condition to maintain and defend the independence of Cuba as well as for its own defense, the Government of the Republic of Cuba will sell or lease to the United States the necessary lands for coaling or naval stations at certain points on the coast to be agreed upon with the President of the United States and on such conditions that they will only serve the military or naval purposes to which they shall be applied".

Wood considered this satisfactory and asked Root's opinion. He replied on the same day that at "first reading", his impression was that "the meaning of the provisions is not changed". He wished, however, to study the matter carefully and to discuss it with the President. He was fearful of new words which would themselves be susceptible of new interpretations and suggested that it would be better for the Convention to adopt the original language and then to add their interpretation.

The majority report was submitted to the Convention on May 24th and proposed the literal acceptance of the Amendment with the addition of certain interpretations.

These interpretations were, in effect, those given by Root to the Cuban Committee and expressed in the various letters to General Wood. As presented by the Committee they emphasized the fact:

". . . . 1st: That the stipulations contained in clauses 1 and 2 of the Platt Amendment are internal constitutional limitations which do not restrict the power of the Government of the Republic of Cuba to freely celebrate political or commercial treaties with any nation, its power to contract loans or create debts only in so far as it must abide by the provisions of the Cuban constitution and the statements made in the beforementioned clauses. 2nd: That the intervention will in no manner imply intermeddling or interference in the affairs of the Cuban Government; it will only be exercised by a formal act of the United States Government for the preservation of Cuban independence and sovereignty whenever threatened from without, or for the establishment in accordance with the constitution of the Republic of Cuba, of a government adequate for discharging its internal and international purposes, in case a real state of anarchy should exist. . . ."

Secretary Root cabled on May 28th that he did not think this constituted a proper acceptance of the Platt Amendment authorizing "the President's withdrawing the army from Cuba". He explained his views in a personal letter of the same date to Wood in which he made the following comments:

"I do not wish to enter into a controversy as to the correctness of the Committee's recollection of the particular expressions which they have gathered or condensed from the long and informal conversations which we had about the

FORMING TREATY RELATIONSHIP 97

provisions of the amendment. The statements in the recitals are, in many respects, inaccurate. The propriety of the use which the Committee are proposing to make of the conversations may be judged by reference to the fact, which you will remember, that what I said was accompanied by the explicit and distinct statement that I had no power or authority to change or modify the law enacted by Congress, and that, whatever I might say, the provisions of that law as they appeared in the statute must be the guide of the President's action; that the only point upon which they desired any formal or authoritative assurance was as to the effect of the third clause relating to intervention, upon which they asked for a written memorandum, and volunteered the statement that, if given, it would be treated as personal to themselves and confidential; that even this I did not give, but that, after saying to them that I could not change or modify the law by anything which I said as to its effect, I procured for them a letter from Senator Platt, stating his views as to the effect of the third clause, which I handed to them marked 'Confidential', and the substance of which has been put into the proposed recitals as coming from me; that as to the so-called despatch of March 29th, mentioned in the recitals as having been referred to by me, which was in fact a personal letter from me to you, the precise extent to which the President was willing to give to the matter contained in that letter an official and authoritative character has been defined and made certain by the despatch of April 3d, also referred to in the recitals.

"I do not think that any part of these recitals of conversation ought to form any part of the resolution to be adopted by the Convention...."

On June 1st Wood cabled that he concurred in these views. He explained that the Committee had resorted to these interpretations despite positive assurances to the contrary in order to obtain the passage of the bill by the narrow margin of fifteen votes to fourteen. There was some further exchange of views, and it was made clear to the Convention that there must be a full acceptance of the Platt Amendment without change. Such acceptance was given on June 12th by sixteen votes to eleven.

Although the United States Government refused to accept, for the reasons stated by Root, the long exposé of the meaning of the Platt Amendment, there does not seem to be much doubt that Root and the Cubans understood that Article III provided for intervention only in case of an anarchical condition in Cuba or in case of foreign invasion. Entirely aside from the conversations in Washington, Root's official and public interpretation sent on April 2, 1901, is clear on this point.

The Cuban opposition to the Platt Amendment was centered almost wholly on Article III. There was hardly a reference to Article II, dealing with finances, which in later years became as much as Article III the object of invocation by the United States. The remaining articles have caused little, if any, difficulty in the relations between the United States and Cuba.

. . . . .

On the 20th of May, 1902, General Wood presented a letter from the President of the United

FORMING TREATY RELATIONSHIP 99

States, Theodore Roosevelt, to "the President and the Congress of the Republic of Cuba" declaring that the occupation of Cuba by the United States was at an end. Tomás Estrada Palma, President of the Republic of Cuba, accepted the government from General Wood, assuming the obligations of the Treaty of Paris which the United States had undertaken in respect of Cuba.

At last the long anticipated day had come when the destinies of the Pearl of the Antilles were in the hands of the Cubans. As President Palma took his oath of office, General Máximo Gómez, with deep emotion, said, "I believe now we have arrived." The crowds in the streets of Havana gave vent to their feelings in laughter and tears, in embraces, shouts of joy, and improvised dancing, with a spontaneous enthusiasm and an overwhelming emotion which is Cuba's heritage from a passionate race nurtured in a burning sun. Throngs lined the waterfront before El Morro, the historic castle that commands the entrance to Havana harbor. The people had come to mingle with free fellow countrymen and to witness the crowning event of their history—the raising of the Cuban flag over El Morro. An American eye witness told me that the American flag on its descent did not run freely, so there was a momentary pause and the flag started up again for a few feet. A skeptic in the crowd said in bewilderment: "I knew it was all a trick! See, the American flag is not coming down!"

But it did come down, and Cuba was free—free at least from the chains, if not from the influences of her colonial past.

Formal diplomatic relations began between the two sovereign countries, Cuba and the United States. At first the Missions at Washington and Havana were of the grade of Legations; in 1923 they were raised to Embassies. On May 20, 1902, H. G. Squiers was appointed American Minister to Cuba and it was his first important duty to conclude a treaty with Cuba in accordance with Article VIII of the Platt Amendment. This was not accomplished without further objection from Cuban officials. Both President Palma and his Secretary of State argued that the rights accorded to the United States in the Platt Amendment should be more narrowly defined in the Treaty, particularly Article III. The Platt Amendment was a very unpopular political issue in Cuba. Secretary Hay, however, emphatically stated the position of the United States Government, that the Platt Amendment was already the law of the land in the United States and Cuba and was not to be modified by the Treaty. At the end of 1902 he transmitted, through the Legation, a draft of a permanent treaty, which merely reproduced the language of the first seven articles of the Amendment. It was finally signed in Havana on May 22, 1903, but the Senate of the United States did not consent to ratification until March 22, 1904 and the ratification of Cuba was not effected until June 20, 1904. Ratifications were exchanged, and the treaty came into force on July 1, 1904.

The Platt Amendment established the basis for the new political relationship that was to exist between the United States and Cuba, but the basis for commercial relations also had to be settled. After nearly four hundred years of foreign rule Cuba, although a free Republic, was not free of tariff barriers against her products. Some of our statesmen of the period evidently recognized that political freedom without a concomitant ability to dispose of her products might not mean salvation to "a country so small as Cuba, so incapable, as she must always be, to contend by force against the great powers of the world."

When the Platt Amendment was being discussed with the Committee of the Constitutional Convention by Secretary Root, he was asked to include provisions granting favorable trade relations to Cuba. This he was not empowered to grant, but he gave assurance that the Administration would do all in its power to achieve this end. Shortly after the death of McKinley in September, 1901, he kept faith with this assurance by sponsoring adequate legislation for reciprocity in the following statement:

"Cuba has acquiesced in our right to say that she shall not put herself in the hands of any other power, whatever her necessities, and in our right to insist upon the maintenance of free and orderly government throughout her limits, however impoverished and desperate may be her people. Correlative to this right is a duty of the highest obligation to treat her not as an enemy, not at arm's length as an aggressive commercial rival, but with a generosity which toward her will be but justice; to shape our laws so that they shall contribute to her welfare as well as our own.

"Our present duty to Cuba can be performed by the making of such a reciprocal tariff arrangement with her as President McKinley urged in his last words to his countrymen at Buffalo on the 5th of September. A reasonable reduction in our duties upon Cuban sugar and tobacco in exchange for fairly compensatory reductions of Cuban duties upon American products will answer the purpose, and I strongly urge that such an arrangement be promptly made. It would involve no sacrifice, but would be as advantageous to us as it would be to Cuba. The market for American products in a country with such a population, such wealth and purchasing power as Cuba with prosperity would speedily acquire, made certain by the advantage of preferential duties, would contribute far more to our prosperity than the portion of our present duties which we would be required to concede.

"Aside from the moral obligation to which we committed ourselves when we drove Spain out of Cuba, and aside from the ordinary considerations of commercial advantage involved in a reciprocity treaty, there are the weightiest reasons of American public policy pointing in the same direction; for the peace of Cuba is necessary to the peace of the United States; the health of Cuba is necessary to the health of the United States; the independence of Cuba is necessary to the safety of the United States. The same considerations which led to the war with Spain now require that a commercial arrangement be made under which Cuba can live. The condition of the sugar and tobacco industries in

FORMING TREATY RELATIONSHIP 103

Cuba is already such that the earliest possible action by Congress upon this subject is desirable." [18]

In Cuba a campaign was initiated to procure favorable trade relations with the United States. In the spring of 1901 a Cuban Commission of planters and merchants was sent to Washington to accomplish this purpose. However, because of the uncertainty then prevailing as to the political relationship that was to exist between the two countries, little progress was made. Wood late in April came to the United States and actively assisted the campaign. Meetings and rallies were held in various parts of Cuba to further the project of a favorable reciprocity treaty. Toward the end of November a group of Cuban merchants, manufacturers, and planters came to Washington and pleaded before the President, important members of the Cabinet and Congress, for economic concessions.

President Roosevelt in his annual message to Congress clearly stated his views of the duty and interest of the United States in the question. He said:

"Elsewhere I have discussed the question of reciprocity. In the case of Cuba, however, there are weighty reasons of morality and of national interest why the policy should be held to have a peculiar application, and I most earnestly ask your attention to the wisdom, indeed to the vital need, of providing for a substantial reduction in the tariff duties on Cuban imports into the United States. Cuba has in her Con-

[18] Report of Secretary of War, Washington, 1901, pp. 47, 48, 49.

stitution affirmed what we desired, that she should stand in international matters, in closer and more friendly relations with us than with any other power; and we are bound by every consideration of honor and expediency to pass commercial measures in the interest of her material well being." [19]

This was the biggest gun fired that year in the perpetual tariff war which we wage on that unsatisfactory battlefield, the lobbies of Congress. Although occasionally harmful to one of the contending armies, this never-ending imbroglio often inflicts much damage on the non-combatants, the American public.

In the battle of 1901 the allied forces opposed to Cuban tariff concessions were the beet sugar producers of the Western States, the Louisiana, Hawaiian and Puerto Rican cane sugar producers, the American tobacco growers and all those who on general principles opposed any tariff reductions lest a precedent be established that might be harmful to their interests. The skirmishes were many and persistent, and the lobbies of Congress were as usual filled with the spies and sharpshooters of the various factions.

That part of the President's message dealing with reciprocity with Cuba was referred to the Ways and Means Committee of the House which opened hearings on the subject. Voluminous and conflicting testimony was taken over a long period. In a report the United States Tariff Commission summarized the de-

[19] James D. Richardson, *op. cit.*, Vol. XIV, pp. 6660-6661.

FORMING TREATY RELATIONSHIP 105

bate by listing thirty-five points on each side of the question.

The arguments in favor of tariff concessions to Cuba were based principally on the following two points:

1. The United States, having assumed responsibility for the political stability of Cuba, should properly secure it; and this stability was dependent primarily upon economic well-being.
2. The Cuban sugar industry was dependent upon the United States as its natural and logical market and could be put on a paying basis only if its product were given free access to that market, necessitating complete exemption or very substantial reduction of import duties.

Opposing arguments pointed out:

1. Some $130,000,000 had been invested in the domestic sugar industry of the United States on the strength of encouragement from the Government and of party pledges, and this investment should be safeguarded by maintaining the policy of protection.
2. Any reduction in the duty on Cuban sugar would be an interference with the existing protection of the sugar industry of the United States, would deprive investors of the incentive for its further development, driving capital to the Cuban industry.

Incidentally, in developing this argument the opponents made the striking admission that "Cuba could produce all the sugar the United States required and more cheaply than any other part of the world."

The Congress was protectionist, and it was only after months of pressure by the Administration, a growing public demand for action, and a threatened split in the party that in March, 1902, Chairman Payne of the Ways and Means Committee of the House introduced a bill authorizing the President to negotiate a commercial arrangement conceding a reduction in duties of 20 per cent. effective to December 1, 1903.

But the opponents of the bill artfully injected the Morris Amendment to repeal the special protection for refined sugar. This insured hostility in the Senate where the sugar refining interests were powerful, and the bill passed the House only to be smothered in the Senate by other important measures, routine business, and the sugar lobby. On July 1st, the Congress adjourned without final action. A prophecy of the people's representative from Michigan had been fulfilled. He had calmly declared after voting for the amended bill:

"Our motive was to kill that bill. That is the plain English of it, and I believe it did kill the bill. I believe that bill will never come back to this House, or if it does come back, it will come in such shape that its author will never recognize it, and I believe that the Senate of the United States will in good time kill that bill and that it will never be resurrected. If the gentleman from Ohio desires to pronounce a

FORMING TREATY RELATIONSHIP 107

funeral oration over the remains of his deceased friend, the Cuban reciprocity bill, we shall raise no objection 'because Bill is dead.' "

In the meanwhile Cuba was suffering great distress from lack of trade, a depleted treasury and burdensome taxation to pay the bills of our administration of Cuba. With the Congress adjourned and temporarily quiescent, President Roosevelt, under his constitutional authority, immediately started negotiations for a Reciprocity Treaty with Cuba. And coincidentally he made an appeal to the people of the United States over the heads of Congress in a speech in August, 1902, when he said:

"Cuba must always be peculiarly related to us in international politics. She must in international affairs be to a degree a part of our political system. In return she must have peculiar relations with us economically. She must be in a sense part of our economic system. We expect her to accept a political attitude toward us which we think wisest both for her and us. In return we must be prepared to put her in an economic position as regards our tariff system which will give her some measure of the prosperity which we enjoy." [20]

Under the ægis of President Roosevelt the treaty was prepared by representatives of the two countries and was submitted to the Senate on December 17, 1902, and approved on March 28, 1903. However,

[20] Theodore Roosevelt, *Addresses and Papers* (W. F. Johnson, Ed.), N. Y., 1909, p. 61.

the treaty contained a provision which necessitated its approval by both Houses. The President called a special session of Congress on November 9, 1903, in order to expedite the passage of the Cuban Reciprocity Treaty which he declared was "demanded not only by our interest but by our honor". Within a little over a month the bill passed both Houses; and on December 17th the President signed it and proclaimed the treaty which went into effect on December 27, 1903.

Under the terms of the Reciprocity Treaty, articles on the free list in either country at the time of ratification would continue to be free, even though subsequent tariffs should make them dutiable when coming from other countries. The United States made a 20 per cent. concession on dutiable articles when they were "the product of the soil or industry of the Republic of Cuba", and Cuba made a similar concession, ranging from 20 to 40 per cent., on behalf of the United States. There was one interesting exception to these provisions; namely, that "Tobacco, in any form, of the United States or of any of its insular possessions, shall not enjoy the benefit of any concession or rebate of duty, when imported into the Republic of Cuba".

In the minds of many this commercial treaty was insufficiently liberal to Cuba in view of the political bonds which linked her with the United States. Nevertheless it gave Cuba more advantages in the American trade than those held by any other country. During the first years in which the treaty was in force Cuba definitely benefited from her 20 per cent. reduction below the established United States tariff on sugar. In this period the United States' demand for sugar absorbed not only Cuba's output, but also imports from other countries. Consequently the New York price of sugar tended to be fixed by the world price plus the full duty, and Cuba was able to profit on account of her duty reduction. Cuba tended to lose the benefit of the price differential, however, when her output exceeded the United States' demand, and imports from other countries ceased. The world price plus the Cuban duty then tended to become the New York price. So today Cuba has indeed a preferred market, but not necessarily a preferred price, for her sugar.

PART III

The Influence of the United States on Economic Development in Cuba

The special condition created by both the Reciprocity Treaty and the Permanent Treaty favored the economic penetration of Cuba by American capital, but there were other factors at least equally influential upon American investment. Havana is about one hundred miles from the tip of Florida, and the time necessary to span this short distance has been steadily reduced until today, at the speed of air travel, only thirty minutes separate the two countries. Also, sugar is the chief source of the wealth of Cuba, and the United States is the world's largest consumer of sugar. The glorious winter climate of Cuba and the educational and cultural opportunities in the United States stimulate a two-way travel between these countries. And Cuba, the gateway to the Americas, symbolized in her coat of arms which portrays a key set between Florida and Yucatan, is by nature placed to participate in the ever growing inter-American traffic of goods and ideas.

The economic condition of the Cubans at the be-

ECONOMIC DEVELOPMENT 111

ginning of this century has been succinctly described by Jorge Mañach, a contemporary Cuban author of great penetration:

"Throughout the first three-quarters of the past century, the Cubans were jealously excluded from public office by bureaucrats brought from Spain. They did, however, own and control the country's economic wealth—land, sugar, cattle, etc. The exploitation of Spanish rule was limited to the enormous taxation levied on this wealth of the Creoles. The campaign of emancipation which began in 1868 obliged the Cuban to sacrifice his connection with that wealth. Plantation owners freed their slaves, saw their sugar mills demolished or burned them themselves, with their own hands; they had to abandon lands and farms to go into the struggle or into exile. The Spaniards took possession in great part of this abandoned wealth. When the Ten Years War ended, therefore, the Cuban had been displaced to large degree by the peninsular Spaniard and by the small group of Cuban 'Tories'. The war of 1895 completed this displacement. When peace was made the Cuban was little less than destitute."

Mañach then points out that Cuba was not a party to the Treaty of Paris and that "the geographic booty—Puerto Rico and the Philippines—was reserved by the United States". He continues:

"Thus emancipation was translated by the American intervention into a semi-subject political independence; and on the economic side the Cuban was left dependent on those who held the island's wealth. These were principally Spaniards. The republic made its debut under the sign of that disappointment. The relationship contracted with the United States opened a wide door for the investment of northern capital. The Cuban was needy. Intervention had damaged him psychologically; he lacked capacity for resistance and decision. He sold a great part of his lands at the first favorable offer, thus opening the way for the monopolization of them by American capital. The population of Cuba was divided into a small privileged class possessing the residue of colonial opulence, and the middle and lower classes, cut off from all wealth." [1]

The statement of facts is enlightening, but the inference is perhaps in a measure distorted—understandably so in view of Cuba's plight at that time.

At the end of the Spanish American War, as Mañach states, "the Cuban was little less than destitute". Foreign and principally American capital, at first slowly, but persistently, flowed into the country to develop her resources. This movement, quickened by the treaties, was nevertheless not the result of any special concessions or privileges, but was brought about by natural causes. Cuba needed banks, highways, railroads, steamships, modern machinery for sugar and other purposes, to enable her industries to compete in the world market; she needed seeds, roots and live stock; all so that she might utilize her natural resources and find a desirable place among the industrial and agricultural countries of the world.

[1] "The Revolution in Cuba," *Foreign Affairs*, October, 1933, pp. 52-53.

ECONOMIC DEVELOPMENT 113

The foreign investor in Cuba drove as good a bargain as he could in accordance with the "profit motive" which has been and is destined to be the impelling force in the world's economic system until human nature has progressed beyond present indications. At the end of the Spanish American War it has been estimated that about fifty million dollars of American capital was invested in Cuba. In 1906 the investment was estimated at $120,000,000 and by 1912 it had reached $220,000,000. During the time of the greatest inflation American capital in Cuba was estimated to be between one and a quarter and one and a half billion dollars. Today this investment may be worth but a fraction of this amount.

Some of these investors have become rich, others have been ruined. But regardless of the individual success or failure of the foreign investor, Cuba, which was "little less than destitute" in 1898, without any of the so-called benefits of modern civilization, today has highways, railroads, electric roads, docks, airways, parks, public buildings, power plants, great and modern sugar factories, industrial plants, a great surplus of poultry and cattle—in short, an accumulation of national assets that constitute a wealthy nation. Between 1898 and the peak of war time prosperity Cuba's international trade increased ten fold and farm land values rose more than a hundred fold.

Many Cubans undoubtedly "sold out" to the shrewd investor from the North who foresaw the possibilities in a Cuba with capital and political stability. And yet, without this stability and capital the land values would have remained stationary.

A general criticism of foreign economic penetration is found in the following typical complaint:

> "These [foreign] banks and companies have no interest in community life, in social conditions in Cuba, other than that which may be inspired by their balance sheets or dividends."

This points to one of the underlying disadvantages, based on abuses of a former epoch, in the use of foreign capital for developing the resources of a country. It is true that the impelling motive of the foreign company is a desire for profits. Nevertheless, enlightened self-interest and an example from industrial practices in the North have caused the foreign capitalist to lead the way in Cuba in providing for better working and living conditions. During the days of the sugar boom, known to Cubans as the days of the *vacas gordas* (the fat cows), real wages in Cuba rose to a point far higher than those in other countries of Latin America, and in fact compared favorably with those in the United States. To make up for the shortage in the labor supply, the Cuban Government permitted the immigration of thousands of natives from Haiti and Jamaica. With the collapse of the sugar market, this proved disastrous for Cuban labor which in recent years has been reduced to a state of

ECONOMIC DEVELOPMENT 115

dire poverty. This practice of importing labor was not confined, however, to the foreign capitalist, but was universal on the island and was partially a result of the native Cuban's dislike during good times to cut cane. A Cuban popular song testifies to it; *Yo no tumbo la caña; que la tumbe el viento*—(I don't cut cane; let the wind blow it down).

There have been instances where American business men, like Cuban business men, have resorted to the vicious practice of attempting to influence the Cuban Government by campaign contributions or by the bribery of public officials; there have been similar instances in the history of our own country. This practice has, of course, been one of the cankerous sores on the body politic of democracy and capitalism everywhere. Those Americans who have engaged in it in Cuba have cast discredit upon their honorable compatriots; but they have neither deserved nor received the support of their own government. Culpable investors will argue that the only way that they can get justice and maintain their rights is by bribery. This is a lame excuse, to which the obvious retort is that under such circumstances they better go elsewhere with their capital.

The impetus which foreign capital gave to Cuban industry and agriculture is similar to that which it gave to the United States and Canada in their pioneering days. This method of development has been generally followed in the undeveloped countries of

Latin America and indeed other parts of the world.

The foreign capital in Cuba penetrates the whole economy of the island. The common carrier railroads of Cuba are almost wholly divided between two companies, one American and the other English owned. Practically all of the ships trading with the island are under foreign flags. These are principally American and English, but include the ships of Spain and other European nations and Japan. The air transportation both on and from the island is wholly American. The cables and wireless are American and English, although the local telegraph service is owned by the Cuban Government. The street railway system is American. The electric light, power and gas works are American. The principal mines are American owned. The sugar industry is roughly 70 per cent. American, 10 per cent. Canadian and English, and 20 per cent. Cuban. In addition, many of the sugar companies are heavily mortgaged to the foreign banks in Cuba.

Aside from a few comparatively small banks which are controlled by Cuban capital, the banks of the island are American and Canadian. They are branches of leading New York, Boston, Montreal, and Toronto institutions, which maintain offices throughout the island, about twenty-eight such offices being operated by three American banks and about thirty-six by three Canadian banks.

Mortgages, exclusive of those on sugar properties,

ECONOMIC DEVELOPMENT 117

are principally held by Cubans and Spaniards. The bonds of the Cuban Government are held almost entirely in the United States.

The life insurance companies are mainly Canadian, only a few relatively small American companies participating in this field; but American companies place a large part of the fire and other insurance in the island.

The cultivation of tobacco, an important Cuban product, is largely in the hands of Cuban citizens, but Spaniards also play no small part in this industry. The manufacture of tobacco is now chiefly controlled by Cubans and Spaniards, the American companies which dominated the manufacturing branch having transferred most of their operations to the United States in recent years.

Two-thirds of the oil business belongs to American companies and one-third to English companies. An American company operates the only petroleum refinery in Cuba.

The packing business is American. Cattle raising is principally Cuban, but there are some American ranchers. Fruit and vegetable farming is mainly Cuban, but there are American farms of importance on the island and on the Isle of Pines. The great majority of the small merchants throughout the island are Spanish, but there are also many Chinese from the large Chinese colony in Cuba numbering about thirty thousand.

Seventy per cent. of the Central Highway was built by an American concern and thirty per cent. by Cuban contractors. An American contracting firm, long established in Cuba, constructed many of the public buildings, including the Capitol, and most of the larger hotels and office buildings, while an American engineering firm built the principal port works in Havana and other cities.

The two leading hotels and some smaller ones in Havana are American owned, but several hotels of importance are owned by Spaniards, and natives of Spain also operate many of the numerous cafés and restaurants. A number of the moving picture theatres are controlled by American companies.

In Cuba the foreign ownership is accentuated for two reasons. First, because the island's natural resources and geographical position have attracted a proportionately larger investment of foreign capital than in other countries. Second, because the stores and small businesses throughout the island are not owned by Cubans, but by Spaniards. This is a tradition that has persisted from Spanish colonial days. In recent years there have been some four or five hundred thousand Spaniards in Cuba out of a total population of four millions. Thus, most of the little business is in the hands of the Spaniards, and the big business is largely in the hands of the Americans, English and Canadians.

This condition is not the result of any Machiavel-

ECONOMIC DEVELOPMENT 119

lian schemes of the American Government or of American business "imperialists", as certain misinformed Cubans and some of the more emotional American commentators report. It is indeed unfortunate for both nations that the Cuban is not owner and manager of the big business and little business of his country, but it is manifestly unjust to put the blame for this on the foreigner whose capital the Cubans sought and needed. There is every opportunity for free competition. This applies equally to big business and to the small business of the Spanish *bodeguero* or storekeeper. The foreign investment in Cuba was a gradual process, not a sudden dispossession, and it was ready to provide business opportunity for the Cuban. The Cubans, however, aspired to the Spanish rôle of wealthy landlord. They had little inclination to achieve this ambition through the slow pains-taking methods—long apprenticeship to small businesses and devotion to work—undertaken as a rule by the modern capitalists of North America and European countries.

Unfortunately, also, the Spanish Colonial Government of Cuba taught the lesson that to the rulers of the land belongs the budget. Since the Cubans became rulers, they have concentrated on the budget instead of business as a means of livelihood. Mañach contends that they "attacked the only resource left to them—the government budget". It might be more accurate to say that this was the most alluring resource—the "easy money" for which everything else was abandoned. Under the influence of this Spanish tradition, the Cuban chose politics as a career and, where possible, entered a profession, especially that of law or even medicine or engineering, as a preparation for it.

This was well expressed by Cuba's philosopher, Dr. Enrique José Varona, as long ago as 1915 in the following quotation.

"To govern the republic, to administer her provinces and municipalities, to increase from year to year her budget, to multiply the number of those who live at the expense of the public treasury; to this the greater part of our activity has been directed. The number of the employees of the subventioned Cubans increase and increase; but the number of small and medium sized rural property owners, of the small and medium sized Cuban merchants do not increase in equal proportion. Our tendency is to live on the budget, not on the soil. . . . We have secured the political independence of the country. It is a great duty that we have accomplished. Another remains. To secure by well directed work the economic independence of the Cuban." [2]

There are, of course, exceptions to this rule, and they indicate a brilliant commercial future for the Cubans when the curse of politics has once been lifted from that bewitched land. The Cuban business man, whether he be sugar planter or industrialist, need yield to no one in ability. He is shrewd, energetic,

[2] *Op. cit.*, "Mirando Adelante," p. 268.

ECONOMIC DEVELOPMENT 121

enterprising, adaptable and tenacious, and he is a good organizer and administrator. If he is perhaps more excitable than his northern prototype, he offers the appealing characteristics of charm and kindliness. Although the foreigner may control the larger share of the business of the island, the outstanding individual successes have been made by Cuban business owners and administrators.

. . . . .

The penetration of American bankers in Cuba presents a little different problem from that of other investors. There are at present only six important commercial banks operating in Cuba, of which three are Canadian and three are American, all branches of large institutions in their respective countries; and in addition there is one important private Cuban bank of Spanish origin. Only one of these banks, an American institution, has directly floated loans for the Government. Formerly there were numerous Cuban and Spanish banks which have closed their doors over the long period of Cuba's deep depression that started several years before our own. There was, as well, the Cuban National Bank which failed as a result of malfeasance and the collapse in sugar prices after the boom.

There is a feeling in Cuba that to the banks is due much of the blame for Cuba's economic ills. Since the economic system has worked badly in recent years and since the banks have been dominant factors in that system, there is reason for criticism. Some bank officials have attempted to profit through personal transactions which violated their fiduciary trust relationship with their clients and stockholders; they have over-capitalized companies, over-loaned, and encouraged over-production; and for all of this their judgment, and in some cases, their probity, are censurable. This conduct of certain bankers has cast discredit on the whole system. In Cuba, unfortunately, foreign bankers are about the only ones left to answer the charges.

One of the three American banks, and the Canadian banks had many large sugar accounts which, with the collapse of the sugar boom, compelled them to take over a great many plantations. This has caused the general impression, not without some reason, that the foreign bankers have a "grip" on the sugar business. What is not generally realized is that this "grip" was unsought, and is both unpleasant and unprofitable. The banks have already written off millions of dollars of bad loans, which they had made because of their optimism and poor judgment in granting excessive credit to Cuban sugar planters; and they were therefore forced to take over a large part of the sugar business by foreclosure.

Another criticism directed against the foreign banks is that they are not liberal enough with their loans to the Cuban. Perhaps now the pendulum has swung too far in the direction of caution, as it has in the United States. But Cuba's ills in the past have been the result not of too little credit, but of too much. The best defense against ungenerous bankers is free competition which banks have enjoyed to the full in Cuba, with few survivals. Cubans have suffered chiefly, just as we have in the United States, from too many banks born of inadequate legislation for the protection of the depositor.

There is some sentiment in Cuba in favor of the establishment of a new National Bank, and some day such a bank will probably take its place in the economic structure of the island. But Cuba's national pride had best be swallowed until such time as there is complete and universal confidence in the ability, experience, and integrity of a board of bank governors. The Bank of England's success could not have been achieved without those qualities in its directors. If in recent years there had been in Cuba a National Bank with the power of note issue, the country today would probably be flooded with depreciated paper currency, and the credit of Cuba, which, in spite of all her troubles, has remained extraordinarily high in comparison with many other countries, would have collapsed completely. In the face of her economic difficulties she could not have maintained any semblance of national credit which is a prerequisite to economic recovery in any nation.

The function of making loans to a foreign government is, of course, distinct from the ordinary commercial banking mentioned above. The history of American loans to Latin America during our orgy of prosperity is a chapter of crass stupidity, unfortunately disclosed by hindsight rather than by foresight. In addition, the chapter reveals at times rapacity and dishonesty which even took the form of bribery by a few bankers to obtain business.

Many of these difficulties might have been avoided if bankers and governments had heeded the warning of ex-President Hoover in 1927 when, as Secretary of Commerce, he addressed the Third Pan-American Commercial Convention as follows:

". . . . I wish to emphasize for your consideration . . . that no nation as a government should borrow or no government lend and nations should discourage their citizens from borrowing or lending unless this money is to be devoted to productive enterprise.

"Out of the wealth and the higher standards of living created from enterprise itself must come the ability to repay the capital, together with the net gain, to the borrowing country. Any other course of action creates obligations impossible of repayment except by a direct subtraction from the standards of living of the borrowing country and the impoverishment of their people.

"In fact if this principle could be adopted between nations of the world, that is, if nations would do away with the lending of money for the balancing of budgets for purposes of military equipment or war purposes, or even that type of public works which do not bring some direct or in-

ECONOMIC DEVELOPMENT 125

direct productive return, a great number of blessings would follow to the entire world.

"There could be no question as to the ability to repay; with this increasing security capital would become steadily cheaper, the dangers to national and individual independence in attempts of the lender to collect his defaulted debts would be avoided; there would be definite increase in the standard of living and the comfort and prosperity of the borrower.

"There could be no greater step taken in the prevention of war itself. This is perhaps a little further toward the millennium than our practical world has reached and I do not propose that these are matters that can be regulated by law or treaty. They are matters that can be regulated solely by the commercial and financial sentiment of each of our countries, and if this body may be able to develop the firm conviction, develop the understanding that the financial transactions between nations must be built upon the primary foundation that money transferred is for reproductive purposes, it will have contributed to the future of the Western Hemisphere in a degree seldom open to a conference of this character."

I was a delegate to this convention and heard the address. It met with little approval, and was condemned by many bankers and Pan-American delegates as unworkable idealism.

Cuban Government loans issued by American bankers have been the subject of much controversy and criticism. This was particularly true during the final years of the administration of President Machado, primarily because in the midst of a devastating depression in which the Cuban Government salaries had been greatly reduced and were constantly four or five months in arrears, comparatively large sums of money were exported to pay interest and sinking fund on the foreign debt. There were two motives for continuation of payments apart from the traditional one of national honor: (1) the maintenance of Cuba's credit, without which reconstruction after the end of the world depression would be extremely difficult and the stress would continue for an undue period after world revival; (2) the historic fear in Cuba that default on the foreign debt would cause the interposition of the United States Government and add to the political perplexities.

The Government employees and politicians were clamoring for a suspension of debt payments, so that they might obtain more funds from the regular budget. Members of the opposition were also demanding suspension, but from a different motive; they hoped that this might cause the interposition of the United States Government and embarrass the Machado Administration. In the higher interests of the Cuban people, as well as in justice to foreign bondholders, it would have been wise to have carried out a refunding plan that would have spread amortization payments on a part at least of the foreign debt over a long period of years. This would have relieved the financial pressure on Cuba and at the same time, would have preserved her credit. Although I suggested such

ECONOMIC DEVELOPMENT 127

a plan to both the Cuban Government and the American bankers, it was rejected on account of the perplexities of the political situation, and in accordance with our policy of strict non-interference the matter was not pursued.

There is a widespread misconception that to the banks are owed the millions of dollars that have been loaned to Cuban and other Latin American Governments. The banks negotiated these loans, and offered the major portion to the American public, who are the real sufferers in case of default. On a few occasions the banks were unable to find purchasers among the public for the bonds, and so have reluctantly been forced to hold them in their portfolios.

Another criticism is that the bankers want stability at all costs and often over-loan to protect their original loans and so bolster up unpopular rulers. This is undoubtedly a fair criticism. But if the Cuban Government borrows money to develop the country's resources, the Cubans must not complain too bitterly because the creditors would rather make limited extensions of credit than permit a default, with its disastrous consequences. The fact that American loans to Latin America are not necessarily either the cause or the effect of dictatorship is best indicated by the case of Venezuela. This is the only country in Latin America in which a dictator has survived the depression, and it is the only country that does not owe a dollar abroad.

The problem of Government loans in Cuba is particularly delicate due to the fact that such loans are governed by the Permanent Treaty between that country and the United States. Under Article II the Cuban Government recognizes the obligation that she "shall not assume or contract any public debt to pay the interest upon which and to make reasonable sinking-fund provision for the ultimate discharge of which the ordinary revenues of the island, after defraying the current expenses of government, shall be inadequate". This imposes a responsibility which leads at times to confusing and difficult consequences for the United States.

While I was in Cuba, for example, rumors were continually circulated regarding prospective American loans to the Machado Government. Several years previous to my arrival in Cuba, the Government had inaugurated a public works program comprising the building of a Central Highway from one end of the island to the other, a Capitol building, hospitals, parks, and other projects. Just before I assumed my post in Havana negotiations were under way between the Cuban Government and American bankers for refunding $40,000,000 of special Public Works Certificates and for borrowing an additional $20,000,000 to complete the highway and other projects. I informed the Department of State after an exhaustive study of Cuban finances that their status was such

ECONOMIC DEVELOPMENT 129

that in my opinion our Government "would not be justified in raising objection to the proposed loan". The revenues pledged for this financing were then much more than adequate for the purpose.

At the same time I informed the Department: "I attach great importance to the fact that a marked curtailment in, or the suspension of, the work in progress on the Central Highway would tend to aggravate the serious economic depression now afflicting the country; and would not only postpone the realization of the economic benefits to be derived from the Central Highway as a finished unit, but might also lead to serious deterioration in the work that has not yet been completed". The road was being built in sections from different points on the island, so that this long anticipated and costly highway would be of no use until the sections were joined together. In other words, without twenty million dollars more there would be no highway.

Later, revenues began declining rapidly in Cuba as they did in the United States. At the same time the Machado Government desired to contract additional loans. After the Public Works refunding operation referred to was consummated, and after the issuance by the Government to the contractors of $20,000,000 of Treasury obligations for bills already rendered, I opposed every proposal to increase the Government's public indebtedness.

In the development of a new country's resources, after the initial impetus given by foreign investment, the nationals tend to acquire the business and conduct its expansion. A fair-minded analysis of the results of American economic penetration of Cuba would indicate that in spite of abuses, the country has greatly benefited by it. A point has now been reached in Cuba's economic development, however, where it would seem most desirable both for Cuba and for the United States, if Cubans would increase their participation in the island's business. This condition can only be realized gradually and with tolerance and understanding on both sides. The time is especially opportune for a change of this sort, on account of present deflated values.

This transition cannot be accomplished, however, if, on the one hand, American capitalists assume that Cuba is to be exploited in the interests of American citizens by the might of their Government, or by the use of bribery and corruption; or if, on the other hand, Cubans assume that the golden country to their north has been placed there by a benign providence for their especial protection; that the capital of the United States should freely flow to Cuba unsecured and without guarantees; and that the products of the soil of Cuba should flow equally freely and unhindered into the United States.

It is interesting to hear from the lips of Joseph

ECONOMIC DEVELOPMENT 131

Stalin, leader and secretary of the Communist Party of Russia the following dictum:

"Our more rapid development of foreign trade depends on conditions and the amount of credit. We have never failed to meet our obligations. We might have claimed a moratorium like the rest of them, but we did not because we did not want to break confidence, and confidence, as everyone knows, is the basis of credit." [3]

In this epoch Cuba cannot survive without capital; capital cannot survive without confidence and protection.

. . . . .

The economic penetration of foreign capital in Cuba finds its fullest expression in the Cuban sugar industry. Since the war this industry in its accumulation of surpluses graphically illustrates a world depression which offered the phenomenon of starvation in the midst of plenty. Those who suffered from a lack of food or clothing were ironically faced with the fact that there was a superabundance of those things in the world. But somehow it could not be utilized. Dr. José I. Rivero, brilliant editor of the *Diario de la Marina,* one of the leading Havana newspapers, epitomized the situation in the following dialogue between a father and his son, sitting in a bare, cold room before an empty hearth:

[3] Interview with Walter Duranty, *New York Times,* 1934.

"Why don't you light a fire, father?"
"Because we have no coal, my son."
"Why have we no coal, father?"
"Because I have no work, my son."
"Why have you no work, father?"
"Because there's too much coal, my son."

This illustrates a condition obtaining in many basic industries. It was particularly true of sugar and, since sugar is the commodity upon which Cuba's economy depends, the surfeited sugar market of recent years shook the island to its foundations.

Sugar cane, "the sweet stick of the East", is supposed to have been indigenous to India. It did not become an article of household consumption until the middle of the sixteenth century. Almost immediately Cuba became an important sugar producer; today she is aptly called the world's sugar bowl. Her soil, temperature and rainfall, which comes in the right quantities at just the right periods, all combine to make it possible to produce sugar with less human effort in Cuba than in any other place in the world.

The reproduction of sugar cane occurs in two ways: either the roots are left in the ground after the year's crop of cane is harvested, and new shoots or "ratoons" spring up to make a new crop; or else short stalks of cut cane are planted horizontally in furrows. From the "eyes" of the joints of these stalks a new crop rises. The latter method is, of course, the more expensive process. In most countries it is not profit-

ECONOMIC DEVELOPMENT 133

able to "ratoon" for more than a year on account of a diminishing yield, and new planting is then resorted to. In the fecund soil of Cuba ratooning is commonly practised from four to eight years, and I have known of some isolated cases where for over twenty successive years the cane has yielded its sweet gift without more encouragement than a mere cutting of the crop and a little cultivation of the ground each year.

At the time of the Spanish American War, Cuba produced about 350,000 tons of sugar which was approximately a third of her previous maximum production. The United States was then, as she is now, the principal market for Cuban sugar. In the years following independence, Cuban production enormously increased.

The island's dependence upon sugar is indicated by the fact that the sugar crop yields on the average about four-fifths of the national income. Precise data on the national income of any country are difficult to procure, but when account is taken of the vast acreage devoted to sugar cultivation, of the huge amount of capital employed in its production, of the diversified traffic of railroads, ports, and steamships devoted to its transport, and the collateral activities to which the sugar industry has given rise, the high relative importance of sugar in the economy of Cuba is indisputable.

The World War has been considered one of the most important factors in, if not the fundamental cause of, present economic disorder. Certainly the sugar crisis can be directly traced to revolutionary changes in sugar-growing as a result of the war. The annual world production of sugar at the outbreak of the World War had reached a total of a little over 20,600,000 short tons, of which about 53 per cent. was cane sugar and about 47 per cent. was beet sugar. The beet sugar fields were located chiefly in Central Europe, and during the war, these were neglected, so that in the crop year 1919–20 the world sugar production was only a little more than 17,500,000 tons, of which about 79 per cent. was cane sugar and 21 per cent. beet sugar. Outside the war zone, at this time high prices stimulated the production of cane sugar, so that in spite of a decrease of over 3,100,000 tons in total production the output of cane sugar increased nearly 2,900,000 tons. With the end of the war the sugar demand—actual, potential and imaginary—caused sugar growers in practically all countries and particularly those in the war area to compete madly with one another to capture this lucrative business. The price of Cuban raw sugar [4] which had been 2.27 cents per pound in July, 1914, and 4.98 cents per pound in November, 1918, soared to the fantastic figure of 19.25 cents in May, 1920. Then the bubble burst, and the price fell to 4.38 cents per pound within the following six months.

The world-wide policy of increasing duties and

[4] On a cost and freight, New York, basis.

bounties, and fixing quotas, which developed in an effort to mitigate the effects of over-production, actually made the situation worse. Production continued to expand until in 1930–31 there was a total world output of over 32,200,000 tons, of which 59.5 per cent. was cane and 40.5 per cent. beet sugar.

As the principal grower of sugar, producing one-fifth of the world's total, and as a country almost entirely dependent upon its sugar crop, Cuba was the first to suffer from the excessive world supply and the collapse of sugar prices. Its first desperate concern was to retrieve the American market against the inroads which had been made by American insular sugar producers. The United States was the largest absolute sugar consumer in the world, with an extraordinarily high per capita consumption.

The United States' supply of sugar is derived from three sources: first, from beet and cane sugar produced in the States, of which the cane is a small proportion of the total; second, from cane sugar made in the Philippines, Hawaii, Puerto Rico and the Virgin Islands; and third, from Cuban cane sugar.

Significant changes have taken place in the sources of the United States sugar supply. In the five-year period 1922–1926, Cuba supplied 56.2 per cent. of all the sugar marketed for consumption in this country, a ratio even higher than in the two preceding five-year periods, and about twice as high as in 1932, when Cuban sugar accounted for only 28.2 per cent.

of our total. On the other hand, the proportion furnished by our insular possessions increased almost uninterruptedly during a 35-year period, from 14.8 per cent. in the period 1897–1901 to 47.7 per cent. in 1932. In other words, our insular possessions provided us with about 70 per cent. more sugar than did Cuba in 1932. In the meantime, the proportion furnished by producers in continental United States has changed but little, being 23.7 per cent. of the total in 1932, or about the average maintained between 1907 and 1921.

The United States market for Cuban sugar is of course circumscribed by the historic American policy of maintaining a tariff for both revenue and protection. Ever since 1789 every tariff act of the United States has afforded protection to the sugar industry with the exception of the Act of 1890, which admitted sugar free, but protected domestic production through a bounty. In the last thirty-five years the tariff on 96 degree centrifugal sugar has varied from a low of 1.256 cents per pound under the Tariff Act of 1913 to the present highest of all rates of 2.5 cents per pound, under the Hawley-Smoot Tariff of 1930, the rates on Cuban sugar being 20 per cent. less in every instance.

In this period of nearly a century and a half of protection to sugar, vested rights of capital and labor have been built up that require due consideration. The problem of revenues to the United States Gov-

ECONOMIC DEVELOPMENT 137

ernment is also involved in the sugar question, as sugar provides about 25 to 30 per cent. of all customs revenues. On behalf of the Brookings Institution, Dr. Philip G. Wright has prepared an impartial study of the sugar problem which is a refreshing departure from the volumes of necessarily partisan briefs put out by attorneys on both sides of the question. Using the sugar consumption figures and duties prevailing in 1922, Dr. Wright calculates that the United States Treasury received that year $124,500,000 or $1.13 per capita revenue from foreign sugar. But the consumer paid $216, 500,000 or $1.97 per capita more than he would have paid, other things being equal, if there had been no duty on sugar. So the public contributed to the protection of the industry, over and above the amount returned to the public treasury, $92,000,000 or $.84 per capita.

With these figures in mind, Dr. Wright defines the tariff maker's problem as being: "How great a degree of ineffectiveness it is wise in the interest of national self-sufficiency to protect".[5] The sugar question to be answered in the United States is: How much sugar shall we grow in the States, how much shall we purchase from the Philippines, Hawaii, Puerto Rico, and the Virgin Islands which are within our tariff wall, and how much from Cuba? The United States can, of course, very largely control its sugar production by means of its tariff. Aside from

[5] *Sugar in Relation to the Tariff*, N. Y., 1924, pp. 97-99, 132.

economic considerations, however, there are historic and political reasons that in fairness should enter into any regulation of the United States sugar imports. Each of the islands certainly has its just claim upon us. Cuba's claim can perhaps be summarized from a paragraph in Elihu Root's letter of March 2, 1901, to General Wood, when he was urging Cuban acceptance of the Platt Amendment:

"The Cubans should understand that the establishment of the relations indicated in these Congressional resolutions will put them in a position where there will be felt in the United States a kindliness and sense of moral obligation towards them as a people for whom we have in a certain degree made ourselves responsible, and the moral force of that feeling will be immense in compelling the establishment of favourable trade relations . . ."

In giving Cuba her political independence we reserved certain rights looking toward the maintenance of Cuba's stability. If we had guarded her economic welfare as zealously, there would have been less occasion to be concerned about her political stability.

Despite the 20 per cent. preferential which Cuba has enjoyed in the American market, the United States tariff policy has not been sufficiently helpful to the Cuban sugar producer. Its cumulative result over a period of many years has been to keep the American market increasingly for the benefit of domestic, principally island, producers. The increase un-

ECONOMIC DEVELOPMENT 139

der the Hawley-Smoot Act of $\frac{1}{4}$ cent per pound on the duty on Cuban sugar merely added a layer to the tariff wall, which was already too high. It took effect a very short time after I assumed my post in Cuba. Before I left the United States, I discussed the sugar tariff with President Hoover. He was strongly in opposition to the proposed enormous increase of over $1\frac{1}{8}$ cents, and he later told me that in securing a compromise at $\frac{1}{4}$ cent, he had been just to both sides. He added: "However, there will be little consolation in that, because no one is ever grateful for negative blessings." The passage of the law, whatever its values were to the American industry, caused dismay in Cuba where bad times, which had preceded our own depression by several years, had already created a difficult economic situation and pointed the way to a bad political condition.

However, it is problematical whether the tariff increase had any practical effect in view of the surplus sugar stocks then in existence. The fall in the price of sugar due to the world-wide over-production, in which Cuba was a leading participant, was the real root of Cuba's economic difficulties.

· · · · ·

For ten years beginning with 1920 when the sugar bubble burst, Cuba made numerous legislative attempts at sugar control, by various schemes of price fixing, restriction of production, and sugar financing.

None of these schemes was sufficiently successful to warrant its continuance for long. Accordingly, efforts were made to supplement them by an international plan to help the sugar-producing countries. International negotiations failed until in 1930 the Chadbourne plan was devised by those interested in the Cuban industry, and was accepted by Cuba, Java, Germany, Czechoslovakia, Poland, Hungary, Belgium, and later Peru and Jugoslavia. The author of the plan described it as follows:

> "First, we have segregated surplus stocks for orderly marketing over a period of five years. Second, we have placed a rigid restriction upon output in the chief exporting countries of the world so that future output plus annual sales of segregated surpluses, will equal and not exceed consumption. Third, we have secured governmental sanction to control the arrangements made, so that recalcitrants can have no opportunity to take advantage of their fellows."

The plan was an attempt under the capitalistic system to establish an international control over an agricultural product grown in many parts of the world. As such, it has had many critics who have pointed to the somewhat disturbing record of other schemes of that kind. The plan must be regarded, however, as an emergency measure not unlike the much more drastic effort to control agricultural surpluses and raise prices undertaken by the Agricultural Adjustment Administration in our own country in 1933.

The Chadbourne plan was attacked especially on the ground that it favored a special group, in an industry where group interests are extraordinarily numerous and complicated. Coöperation and identity of viewpoint are difficult to obtain in an industry which in Cuba is made up of such diverse elements as the large foreign producer; the large Cuban producer; the small Cuban producer; the foreign refiners who are principally interested in refining and not production; the *colono,* or planter, who cultivates the cane either as a tenant or independent farmer, but who is largely dependent financially upon the mill owner; the laborer—Cubans, Peninsular Spaniards, Canary Islanders, Jamaicans, Haitians and Asiatics; the mortgage-holding banks; the sugar speculator; and, finally, the people. This is merely a glimpse of the patchwork quilt known as the sugar industry, which is too often a subject for glib description by American writers who may spend a few days or weeks in Cuba.

Among these different groups it was to be expected that charges would be made that the plan favored certain interests. Those who attacked the plan charged that it benefited the foreign banks, that it was detrimental to the small mill owners, that it was contrary to the interests of the *colonos,* and that it was another "Yankee trick" to benefit production of sugar within the United States.

In general, it can be stated that at the start the plan had the support of the banks and weakly financed producing companies, and faced the opposition of the American refiners and some of the more strongly financed companies. The banks were "holding the bag" and hoped that the plan would raise prices and reëstablish some value for the sugar properties which they had been financing. The companies without strong financial support anticipated ruin unless prices should rise. On the other hand, the more strongly financed companies would not have objected to the destruction of their weak competitors; and the refiner was, of course, chiefly interested in a large cheap output of Cuban sugar; in fact, the lower the price of raw sugar, the lower the refiner's costs and, other things being equal, the greater the sales of refined sugar; even if the raw sugar is sold below the cost of production, the refiner still makes his profit. The refiner's financial status was strong; he was eager for a battle on the basis of the survival of the fittest; and so he bitterly protested the Chadbourne plan which reduced the output in his mills. In addition, the refiner has an inherent antipathy toward any organization of sugar producers, because he fears that from it may develop coöperative selling which may adversely affect him. The campaign against the Chadbourne plan was originally fought and financed principally by the American refiners.

Regardless of the merits or demerits of the Chadbourne plan, it seems clear that without it, under a policy of *laissez faire,* American ownership in Cuba's

ECONOMIC DEVELOPMENT 143

sugar production would have become nearly complete. The banks had the resources to protect their own interests, and would have done so; the refiners would have protected theirs and probably expanded their business; but only a few Cuban properties could have survived for long in that period of ruthless competition. Before the World War, Americans owned about 35 per cent. of the sugar properties of Cuba, and today they own nearly double that proportion. Some of that increase was voluntary, some involuntary, due to mortgage foreclosures by American banks.

With no improvement in sugar prices and with an increasingly turbulent political situation, the Chadbourne plan became more and more unpopular with the passage of time; most of the attacks developed as it became evident that the hopes and predictions as to a rise in the sugar price would not materialize. In fact, the price of sugar during the time of operation of the plan reached the lowest point in the history of its production, falling from an average price in 1930 of 1.49 cents per pound to 1.38 in 1931 and .92 in 1932 (based on price of 96 ° centrifugal Cuban sugar on New York market, cost and freight).

The opponents of the plan point to the decline in the price of sugar as an evidence of the plan's failure. Of course, during this period the price of all commodities suffered progressive declines in price with the deepening of the world depression. The opponents further contend that an international plan which does not have the full coöperation of the United States domestic and island producers cannot be effective.

Those who defend the plan declare that the continuing decrease in consumption prevented the hoped-for equilibrium in supply and demand, which the restriction on production was intended to accomplish, and so the benefit of a price rise was not achieved. They also contend that because of the material reduction in output which the plan has effected, sugar is in a far better position than it would have been under free competition, and that the industry will prosper at the first signs of world recovery.

In any event, the Cuban people have continued to protest against the visible result of the plan—a comparatively small crop. The *colono* and the laborer have suffered intensely from a small production, especially as the promised reward of higher prices was not realized. A large production would have meant more money in circulation which appeals to everyone. The community as a whole, however, was not interested in how the sugar was to be sold or even financed. That was someone else's problem. Their suffering had been so great over a long period that they could find no solace in the argument that they might be even worse off if their country had not participated in an international sugar plan which was at least gradually reducing surpluses in spite of a con-

ECONOMIC DEVELOPMENT 145

tinuing depression. The Cuban producer and the *colono* had never before been faced with a condition in which sugar could not be sold at some price. To them this was incomprehensible.

The Chadbourne plan included the issue of $36,973,480 out of an authorized issue of $42,000,000 of bonds to finance the purchase of about 1,320,000 long tons of sugar to be segregated and sold over a period of five years. At the end of the first three years of the plan, about half of these bonds had been redeemed. These bonds were secured by the segregated sugar and guaranteed by the Cuban Government. Although this was in the nature of a commodity loan by a private corporation, its guarantee by the Cuban Government constituted, in my opinion, an obligation under Article II of the Permanent Treaty that demanded consideration by our Government. This is but one of many examples of how this treaty responsibility involves the United States in Cuba's internal affairs, in a manner subject to general misinterpretation. In a despatch to the Department of State on October 14, 1930, considering the Chadbourne plan and its financing, I said:

". . . . the plan provides for the imposition of an additional tax on the entire production of sugar during the life of the bonds . . . The yield of the proposed special production tax could be raised to any point necessary to meet the interest on these bonds and to provide for their amortization in the event that the net proceeds of the sale of the hypothecated sugar should average less than $4.00 per bag. In other words, recourse to the ordinary revenues of the Cuban Government would not become necessary, unless the Cuban sugar industry were seriously impaired by some unforeseen disaster (pests, hurricanes, revolutions, etc.). In this case, there would be a shortage of sugar production in Cuba and there would probably be an increase in the value of the hypothecated 1,500,000 tons. . . .

"The history of stabilization plans does not inspire confidence. In the proposed measure an attempt is being made to avoid some of the difficulties that other plans have encountered. Whether all of the dangers have been eliminated will only be known in the future. But that Cuba is confronted with a crisis there is no doubt; so 'I cannot prefer a certain present evil to a future hypothetical one'."

It will remain for economists and historians of the future to appraise both the short term and long term effects of the Chadbourne plan on the economy of Cuba in particular, and the world in general. Perhaps it will then be considered to have served a purpose as an expedient in an attempt to correct a disorder which could only be permanently corrected by fundamental world economic changes for which mankind was then not sufficiently prepared. We are at present passing through a period when as a result of high tariffs the nations are stressing economic self-sufficiency rather than foreign trade. It may not be far in the future when the pendulum will swing in the opposite direction, toward "freer trade". However, in the economic field the world has departed so far from such a funda-

ECONOMIC DEVELOPMENT 147

mental principle that a sudden attempt to apply it in full would no doubt heap a new disaster upon the present one.

It is perhaps indicative of the advent of a new "economic pattern" that captains of highly protected industries are already willing to see a reduction in tariffs, if not in their own industry, at least in the other fellow's. They are not yet prepared to advocate that each country shall confine its productive activities to those enterprises which it is really fitted to undertake, nor are they confidentially whispering in Congressional ears the classic argument for free trade: "If a great artist also happens to understand cooking, he better devote his time to painting masterpieces and employ a chef to prepare his food". There probably is a growing realization that if the world battle of tariffs, bounties, and quotas continues unabated, it will lead to the *reductio ad absurdum* of each country cut off from all foreign trade living completely within its borders, and the United States, for example, growing sugar cane in greenhouses on the shores of Lake Superior.

The world crisis is bringing social and economic problems squarely before us in an unprecedented way. Their solution can only be found in courageously attacking these problems at their source instead of applying counter-irritants which in the long run merely create new problems. The plain fact of the general sugar problem is that Cuba and Java, which can produce sugar with far less human effort than any other countries, should, for the benefit of mankind, supply a larger part of the world's sugar.

Cuba needs a reasonable share of the United States market for her sugar if her industry is to survive. She needs a quota that will be part of a total that will not oversupply that market. She cannot survive an excessive tariff against this quota. She needs a coördinated sugar industry to take the fullest advantage of her natural resources in sugar and to avoid the harmful consequences of a new blind competition. In a Fourth of July speech in Cuba in 1932 I said:

"In the industrial system the handwriting is clearly on the wall. This is only one of the economic and social problems which await a progressive evolution. . . . We see before us great industries in different parts of the world, under pressure of cut-throat competition and by means of vast financial resources, producing commodity surpluses which they are unable to distribute. The mad production keeps on until their financial resources, great as they are, are exhausted. Then there follows a drastic curtailment in the industry; millions of families are soon faced with ruin, and by their loss of purchasing power carry the germs of depression into every other industry.

"This order cannot persist. There must be a national and international coördination of the units in industries, with adequate protection to the consumer, if we are to prevent the ever accelerating swing of the pendulum from inflation to deflation. It may require some imagination, perhaps, to visualize a world-coördinated industry, steering a steady course between over and under production, with its labor

ECONOMIC DEVELOPMENT 149

safeguarded through temporary slack periods by special reserves and by a judicious application of the so-called "stagger" system which maintains all the labor in any industry by lessening the working hours of the individual laborers. This conception, as I say, may require some imagination, but none is needed to realize that the present order, where millions are either unemployed or insecure in mind, cannot survive and is not worthy of survival."

. . . . .

But the establishment of order in the sugar industry is only a preliminary to certain basic changes in Cuba's agrarian system—changes already considered in the student program for Cuba. The Cuban student movement, as herein discussed, refers to the general reform movement initiated by the youth of Cuba and subsequently adopted by various organizations. It began in the second term of President Machado, and its immediate and passionate objective was the removal of the President from office; but the movement eventually embraced certain sweeping economic reforms, including the breaking up of the huge sugar estates and the creation of a middle class of prosperous farmers.

The need for social and agrarian reform in Cuba is patent. Legislation preventing the creation of the enormous holdings of land, commonly referred to as *latifundia,* might have hindered Cuba from gaining that fabulous wealth which she recklessly enjoyed during the *danza de los millones*—the dance of the millions. And at the same time it would probably have stimulated the growth of a modest self-supporting agricultural country independent, in a measure, of the vicissitudes of world sugar markets and economic cataclysms. Cuba might not have passed through that wild orgy of spending when rich Cuban sugar planters placed large sums on the turn of a roulette wheel; when luxurious palaces sprang up with the speed of suburban bungalows in the residential section of Havana; when flowers were imported from United States greenhouses to give *éclat* to the tables of the rich; when the laborer backed his judgment on the bellicose appearance of a game cock to the extent of the price of a year's subsistence today; when the farmer was so successful planting cane that he couldn't bother to produce even eggs, and one year imported thirteen million dozens largely from the United States. All this was accompanied by an international trade that had risen from $117,000,000 in 1900 to $1,350,000,000 in 1920, with a favorable balance in the latter year of $237,000,000, and a budget which had risen from $16,000,000 in the days of don Tomás Estrada Palma to $130,000,000 in the fiscal year 1920–21.

Cuba might indeed have foregone all this and thus avoided the bitter reaction to her mad dance of the millions. She might have avoided the present plight of closed mansions, mortgaged farms, uncultivated cane fields, warehouses depleted of everything but sugar, run-down railroads, filled-in harbors, unemployment, misery and undernourishment. She might have limited her great money crop, sugar, some years ago; and might have established a system of small farms, producing diversified crops, bringing in little revenue, but supplying domestic needs.

In retrospect, it is very clear that if a policy had been carried out for Cuban economy aiming at this golden mean of Greek philosophy, the utilitarian ideal might have been achieved. But does Cuba want a golden mean and will she choose it for the future? Will she abjure "dancing"? Or will she dance and again pay the piper as she has paid in the past, with her life's blood? Or will she dance and expect Uncle Sam to pay the piper?

The student economic program—indeed, any plan for agrarian reform in Cuba—would depend upon the development and education of a middle class and the very gradual process of land division. These are practical difficulties. The Cuban population is neither prepared nor eager to assume the rôle of independent farmer. The Cuban landowner will offer bitter opposition to any division of his holdings; and compared with this factor, the question of American investments is of relatively little importance. Contrary to the general belief, Americans do not own "most of the island" of Cuba; according to the best estimates available, they own about 30 per cent. of the area, excluding land occupied by urban property, the littoral, swamps and rivers. In its relations with Cuba the United States has maintained an exceptionally good record in refraining from demanding or supporting special privileges for its investors in the island, and hence American landowners would be expected to conform to any agrarian reform fairly instituted and uniformly applied by the Cuban people for their country's welfare. But whether that part of the Cuban people owning the seventy per cent. of the land would agree to this distribution of property is the question.

Aside from this, the success of legislation effecting any such agrarian reform would be particularly difficult at this time when Cuba is facing the profound depression of her sugar industry. Cuba is impoverished under the strenuous competition to sell more sugar than there is a demand for in the United States and world markets; so that any radical reforms that will unduly raise the cost of production of Cuban sugar will complete Cuba's ruin. Also, the experience of other countries in similar movements should be a warning that any such revolutionary program must be economically sound and will require large capital expenditures. Foreign credit for these purposes is only available to a country when there is faith in its finances and its political stability. With a national reorganization of the sugar industry to meet the necessities of the present world order, however, much marginal sugar land might become available for

ECONOMIC DEVELOPMENT 153

homesteading. The abandonment of some of the less profitable sugar lands would be desirable, not only because of the need for crop restriction, but also because of the increasing yields per acre in the sugar industry.

One way of stimulating agrarian reform in Cuba would be to make a careful revision of the archaic tax system which, since Spanish times, has held to its fundamental principle of favoring the landlord.

A complete revision of the tax laws was among the reforms that I urged upon President Machado. I finally succeeded in having Professor E. R. A. Seligman appointed to make a comprehensive report on this subject for the Cuban Government. His international reputation in this branch of economics was such that his findings could not properly be questioned on account of bias. After a comprehensive survey, with the assistance of the various interested elements of the country, and after adequate hearings, the report was delivered to the Government. In his report Professor Seligman said:

> "The tax system of Cuba is largely a heritage of the colonial Spanish system. Like all the continental systems of the later Middle Ages it was dominated by the interests of the mother country and of the large landowners."

In forwarding a copy of the report to Washington, I wrote in February, 1932, on one of the many occasions when I was urging political peace for Cuba:

"With the reëstablishment of moral peace by political compromise, Cuba's finances could be reconstructed so as partially to preserve her credit, and her tax system could be satisfactorily reorganized along the lines of Professor Seligman's report. Unfortunately, however, it is more than likely that the report will be filed with no action taken on it whatsoever, until time has brought about many changes in Cuba."

The first part of this prophecy has been fulfilled as the report was filed by the Machado Administration.

PART IV

POLITICAL ACTIVITIES IN CUBA AND THEIR RELATION TO UNITED STATES POLICY

IN THE short life of the Cuban Republic—only one-third of a century, even less time than is needed for an individual to acquire experience and judgment—that country has learned many lessons and has achieved, in comparison with other countries with similar problems, remarkable progress. This is due primarily to the Cuban's extraordinary intelligence and energy, in spite of the tropical climate in which he lives. It is also due, in my opinion, to the proximity of the island to the United States and to the assistance that Cuba has had from the people and Government of the United States. It is important to realize that most of the examples of Cuban political life which are intermittently brought vividly to the attention of the American public are recurrences of evils initiated in Cuba by Spanish colonial tradition and persisting throughout the history of the Republic.

Reflecting upon the richness of Cuba's soil, the warmth of her sunshine and her island setting, a

Cuban friend once enthusiastically remarked: "If Cuba could have ten years of honorable and moderately wise government, my country would be converted into a veritable paradise". He indicated the chief malady from which Cuba has suffered for four centuries—politics. Her natural riches are so great that in good times she blooms in spite of this affliction, only to wither wretchedly at the first signs of economic stringency.

Political corruption placed its destructive hand on Cuba during the Spanish régime and culminated in the devastation of the island during the prolonged wars for independence. Following the separation from Spain, the chaos and the lack of any experience in democratic government made necessary an American military occupation. Later, after a short period of Cuban administration under the Republic, politics brought again an American intervention. Cuban politics, which has not recognized service to the state as the first principle of statecraft, has been responsible for the malfeasance, the mismanagement, and the revolutions that have been all too frequent in the life of the Republic.

Soon after the establishment of the Republic, politics developed in a manner not unlike that of some of the notoriously corrupt municipal governments of the United States. In 1922 General Crowder, in his capacity as Special Representative of the President of the United States, sent a series of memoranda to

President Zayas urging various political reforms. One of these messages discussed the subject of governmental graft. Some years later, on my appointment as Ambassador to Cuba, General Crowder most courteously and helpfully came to New York to confer about Cuban problems. He said to me at that time: "When I returned from Cuba to Chicago and witnessed the corruption of municipal politics in that city, I felt a sense of shame in recalling that memorandum which I found necessary to send to President Zayas."

Cubans resent our criticism of their political practices in the face of our own unpardonable scandals. Public opinion in Cuba generally fails to distinguish between the few outstanding cases of wholesale dishonesty in municipal politics in the United States and the comparative freedom from it in our Federal Government. The exceptions, such as that of the Teapot Dome scandal, loom high in the Cuban public imagination and are advantageously used by the Cuban politician to condone his own weaknesses and to augment the popular conception of American hypocrisy in public life.

Charles E. Chapman in his thoughtful work on Cuba, referring to the elections of 1922 pointed out that "more than one-fifth of the candidates had penal antecedents. Not only do they accept graft; they solicit it." [1]

[1] Charles E. Chapman, *History of the Cuban Republic*, N. Y., 1927, p. 509.

An old saw which seems to have its application the world over is "Politics makes strange bedfellows". Few countries offer as strange and rapid a realignment of political forces as Cuba. Vital political issues are scarce in Cuba, and elections are fought over personal issues and party affiliations. This condition affords the candidates unusual opportunities for political somersaults. The opposition to the Government, always very bitter, consists of the combined forces of all the defeated candidates. It ceases to be united as soon as it is victorious, however. Then there is a rearrangement of forces, with the new leader finding some of his former allies against him, now on the side of the displaced régime. In the political history of Cuba it has happened again and again that a politician who has barely escaped from Cuba with his life returns after a change of régime in fraternal intimacy with the very politician who sought to destroy him.

A Cuban document of 1923 catalogues the vicious political practices of that epoch, which Chapman summarizes as follows:

"Tax frauds that were forced on people by government officials for the benefit of the latter; the graft in customs collections; the state of abandonment, as well as the corruption, in the affairs of the Public Works Department; lack of attention to sanitation and public charity; the exploitation of lewd women by the higher politicians; the decline in education, and its accompaniment of a rapid increase in illiteracy; the corruption of the judiciary; the use

POLITICAL ACTIVITIES 159

of the army in politics; the glaring remissness of Congress in failing to enact needed laws, and its startling activity in fostering every conceivable form of governmental impropriety; the unconstitutional acts of the President in legislating by decree; and electoral manipulations that tended to keep the power in the hands of those least worthy of possessing it." [2]

Although in the first years of the Machado régime there was a tendency to eliminate some of the evils listed in this formidable indictment of Cubans by Cubans, the murderous feud between the government and students ended in a series of brutal official executions without trial, and a suppression of liberties that greatly exceeded any of the outrages of previous administrations. These excesses contributed decisively to the downfall of the Machado administration; as Carlyle philosophizing on the French Revolution has said: "Most delicate is the mob queller's vocation; wherein too-much may be as bad as not-enough."

In regard to presidential elections Chapman quotes the following comment which he says "hits the mark":

" 'In the history of Cuba no candidate for the presidency has ever lost an election who was backed by the government. [Estrada] Palma reëlected himself to be ousted by a revolution; Gómez, leader of the revolution, who was favored by the intervention government, became president; Menocal was supported by Gómez with the rural guard and defeated

[2] *Ibid.*, pp. 466-467.

Zayas, and four years later he reëlected himself, and in the following election threw the support of the government to Zayas who was declared president by a decision of the supreme court.'"[3]

A Cuban friend facetiously, but philosophically, summed up the inevitable bitter strife for the Presidency, saying: "The trouble with Cuban politics is that there are four million Cubans and only one Presidential office!"

Disorders in the Cuban Republic, including the distressing events during the last half of 1933, are the result of Cuba's immature attempts at democratic government. With the establishment of the Republic the franchise was suddenly bestowed upon the Cuban masses who for centuries had been under the influence of the "twin evil spirits of autocracy and exploitation". The new voter, lacking in general education and politically ignorant, soon became the victim of the politicians. The traffic in votes in Cuban elections has been general. The voter has been taught to believe that he has an inalienable right to sell his vote in a free market, and when that market is closed, as in periods of the suppression of political liberties, he is more sympathetically inclined to revolutionary movements.

The problems of electoral administration in Cuba are, therefore, not altogether problems of method. The Advisory Law Commission during the United

[3] *Ibid.*, p. 567.

POLITICAL ACTIVITIES 161

States intervention of 1906, headed by General Crowder, recommended various electoral reforms which were adopted in 1908. These reforms, the Commission hoped, would "so improve the political habits . . . as to prevent, in great part, a repetition of the same or similar evils in the future". Twelve years later, however, in proposing a new electoral code, Crowder was obliged to confess to the Secretary of State of the United States that:

"Every intent and purpose for which the machinery was created and set in motion in 1907 and 1908, were in the end thwarted, not so much on account of the inherent weakness of the law as such, but on account of the absolute disregard and narrow interpretation of its provisions by those charged with its execution."

Among other reforms, I suggested to President Machado that the Crowder electoral code of 1919 which had been emasculated should not only be restored but completely revised in the light of the experience of both Cuba and the United States in the years since the code was enacted.

. . . . .

Perhaps as a result of the short time that the Cuban people as a whole have had to prepare for democratic government, there are three outstanding and fundamentally destructive abuses that have persisted for many years in Cuban politics.

The first is the abuse of the Cuban National Lottery for the personal enrichment of the politicians in power. The National Lottery is an old Spanish custom which was suppressed during the United States occupation. It was revived in 1909 under the administration of President Gómez. In 1912 an amendment to the lottery law gave the President dictatorial powers over the lottery, with freedom from investigation and audit. Out of this developed the system of graft in the lottery, amounting to a million dollars a year in bad times and to five or six millions in good times, for personal disposal by the President. His "obligations" are many, but his powers of disposal are absolute. This is the recognized illegitimate profit from the lottery and has nothing to do with the Government's legal share of the proceeds from the sale of lottery tickets. In brief, the "racket" is the following: The President indirectly disposes of all lottery tickets to his preferred agents, principally politicians, and fixes a price *above* the legal price, under which no one is permitted to sell. The difference between the legal price and the market price, which varies with the economic condition of the country, is the profit for Cuba's "preferred list". Of course, no one is obliged to buy a lottery ticket above the legal price, or at all for that matter, but most people do.

The distribution of the lottery graft in the time of President Zayas is typical. The Director General of the lottery was the President's son. At that time the income of the two from the collectorships was reported to be about $3,000,000 a year. "Some two hundred collectorships [each valued at over three thousand dollars per annum] were distributed among senators, and two hundred and fifty to three hundred more to members of the House. The average number of collectorships held by senators was about eight, but one senator was known to have sixteen and another fourteen. Not more than two senators had no collectorships at all. The average for representatives was between two and three, but several were known to have six, while there were not more than ten at the outside without any. The remaining six or eight hundred were distributed to various members of the political class." [4]

Every government has its forms of corruption, but the lottery would seem to be a particularly insidious one. The spoils from the lottery contain the putrefying germs that destroy the Cuban body politic. Unless these spoils are removed, there can be no permanent political growth in Cuba.

Another fundamental political abuse in Cuba is the wholesale passage of amnesty laws and the granting of pardons. During the short life of the Republic down to the end of 1931, there were enacted thirty general amnesties, and nearly eight thousand pardons were granted.

Of the amnesty laws, six were in the nature of

[4] *Ibid.*, p. 557.

legislative pardons to specific individuals. None of these laws sets forth the names of the intended beneficiaries, but in five instances only one man was actually in the situation described in the law, and in the sixth instance the law was obviously applicable only to the fraudulent trustees of two savings banks. Of the remaining twenty-four amnesty laws, thirteen related primarily to crimes incident to public disorders (including riots, insurrections and labor troubles); eight absolved those guilty of crimes in the elections and party reorganizations of 1902, 1906, 1910, 1917, 1918, 1927, 1928, and 1930; one, that of 1924, released all those guilty of crimes punishable by imprisonment up to nine years, with the exception of robbery, theft, counterfeiting, and the like; and two, enacted in 1909 and 1910, were sweeping jail deliveries, applicable to practically all crimes punishable by not more than nine years' imprisonment.

Amnesty with respect to acts of a distinctly political character may, of course, be in the highest public interest, but amnesty for common crimes, even if such crimes be in some way connected with political disturbances, cannot fail to have a demoralizing effect upon the administration of justice. The amnesties almost automatically granted for electoral offenses have made a mockery of the electoral codes so carefully drawn by General Crowder, and the jail deliveries of 1909 and 1924 indicated that the Cuban lawgivers were willing to condone the breaking of laws by their fellow citizens.

Grants of executive clemency also helped to undermine the administration of justice. Estrada Palma made a beginning in this respect with 352 pardons. Governor Magoon, whatever may have been the reasons for his action, set an unfortunate precedent by giving 1250 pardons. This number was surpassed by Gómez with 1547 and was more than doubled by Menocal's 2940. Zayas, during his first two years, gave 826 pardons. Unfortunately records are not available indicating the number of pardons granted in the two succeeding years of this administration. Machado resolutely refused executive clemency during the whole of his first administration, but changed that policy beginning in December, 1929. Of the 844 persons who benefited by Machado's clemency during the twenty-five months ending in December, 1931, approximately three-fifths, or 489, were "totally" pardoned, that is, relieved of further punishment; and of these, approximately 400 were serving terms for crimes of violence. In Machado's administration and in those of his predecessors it was noted that the approach of elections was heralded by the release of unusually large numbers of criminals. The prerogative of pardon is undoubtedly, when used with restraint, "the safety-valve of the law". The experience of Cuba is a sad illustration of what it can be when used without restraint.

Closely related to the abuse of amnesties and pardons is a third fundamental abuse, that of the immunity of members of the Cuban Congress. The Constitution of Cuba provides that members of the Congress, unless they are taken *flagrante delicto*, shall be arrested or indicted only with the permission of the body to which they belong. The sense of solidarity and mutual courtesy among Cuban Senators and Representatives is very deep, so deep that the requisite permission for the arrest or indictment of a member of the Congress is almost invariably withheld. In practice, therefore, the personal and political acts of a Cuban Senator or Representative are restrained only by his sense of honor and propriety. The political consequences of the immunity are unfortunate.

For this reason Cuban newspapers and occasionally business organizations have on their staff a member of Congress who takes responsibility for the acts of these organizations and can aid them with his personal immunity. In all the efforts to establish political reforms the greatest resistance was encountered to suggestions for modifying this Congressional immunity.

· · · · ·

The student movement, whatever its weaknesses and ineptitudes, had its origin in a revolt against Cuban political practices and was stimulated by the greed and lack of foresight of the politicians. It is difficult

POLITICAL ACTIVITIES 167

for the North American to comprehend a situation in which the students take such a prominent part in government. When I asked a Cuban friend after the fall of Machado whether the University of Havana, which had been closed for three years would reopen, he answered: "The University will reopen, but I do not know who will attend, as the students are all busy governing."

The North American must understand that the Latin American youth in the past has not found an outlet for his surplus energies and maturing ambitions in athletics and other highly organized student activities, which are such an important part of Anglo-Saxon university life. In addition, the intrigue and conspiracy which dominated Cuban life for centuries were ingrained in the youth of the country. A natural gift for oratory coupled with youth's usual tendency toward radical experiment and change, makes the Latin-American university an incubator for political movements.

Also, there is a Cuban tradition for student martyrdom, that played its part in the recent sanguinary guerrilla warfare between the Machado régime and the students. In 1871, eight students were tried for the offense of violating a tomb in connection with a political incident. They were found guilty after an unfair trial and shot. Their innocence was afterwards pronounced by the Spanish Cortes. Today one of the prominent landmarks of Havana is a fragment of the firing wall against which these students were placed for execution. The wall is now surrounded by a little Greek temple and a tablet bears this inscription:

"On the 27th of November 1871 there were sacrificed in front of this place by the Spanish Volunteers of Havana, the eight young Cuban students of the First Year of Medicine."

The student group has employed as one of the rallying calls the catch phrase—"Yankee Imperialism." Originally this widespread cry was a protest against the extension of the territory of the United States at the expense of Latin America; later, against views such as that of Secretary Olney claiming "the United States is practically sovereign on this Continent, and its fiat is law upon the subjects to which it confines its interposition"; and still later against so-called "dollar diplomacy" and the policy of "preventive intervention". In very recent years with the disappearance of these causes for protests and with the advent of the world depression, there has developed a tendency to direct the fire against the foreigners whose capital is developing the resources of the country. In so far as the protest against "Yankee Business Imperialism" is an attack on the foreign investor, it should take into consideration the present accepted policy stated by former President Hoover, that it "ought not to be the policy of the United States to intervene by force to secure or maintain contracts between our citizens and foreign states and their citizens. Confidence in that attitude is the only basis upon which the economic coöperation of our citizens can be welcomed abroad. It is the only basis that prevents cupidity encroaching upon the weakness of nations—but, far more than this, it is the true expression of the moral rectitude of the United States." [5]

The student protest was also directed against the results of the world depression, and represented an attack on the capitalistic system for which the United States stands as a principal sponsor. That the system has shown signs of disease, and that it must throw off its malady, be root-pruned or be uprooted is the view of enlightenment in the United States, but this view is ignored by the young protestants.

The original objective of the student program was only incidentally the elimination of the absentee owner, but aimed chiefly at reforms in the political and agrarian system which has hampered the growth of Cuba. The absentee owner is a minor obstacle in the path of these reforms, the principal obstacles being the political caste and the resident land owners. However, the student ideology, in which the revolt against President Machado was the first objective, only retained its purity until the overthrow of his régime, when it was forced to engage with the hard realities of practical politics.

The student movement was a manifestation of the

[5] Address before Gridiron Club, Washington, April 13, 1929.

awakening civic consciousness in Cuba. Most of the politicians in former President Machado's government as well as many in violent opposition to it failed to appraise and take advantage of this sign of progress. Instead of political purification, which was Cuba's greatest need, there occurred a bitter internecine political warfare that brought ruin upon the country.

One of the major difficulties in Cuban politics is a reluctance to coöperate or compromise. In the long negotiation which I conducted in 1931 at the request of both the Government and opposition, I sought a compromise that would avoid bloodshed and if possible prevent the revolution that broke out in August of that year. On one occasion I conferred with the principal leader of the revolutionary group, General Menocal, and the following quotation is from a memorandum prepared after the conference: "I pointed out that in the event of an attempted revolution whichever side might win, Cuba would be the loser. Should the Government succeed either quickly or after much bloodshed, in quelling a revolt, hope for political liberties in the future would be lessened; on the other hand, should the opposition win, it would be faced with the serious difficulty of maintaining a government in the face of a tremendous economic depression with counter-revolutionary movements constantly threatening."

The Government, as predicted, did win the revolution, and "political liberties", to put it mildly, "were lessened". At first, both General Menocal and President Machado were willing to compromise, but General Menocal subsequently withdrew his acceptance for reasons which illustrate the difficulties of coöperation in Latin America. In the first place, the gambling instinct urged the opposition to try to get all, even though they might lose all; and, secondly, the fact that their adversary was willing to compromise must indicate a sign of weakness. In addition, they had a filibustering expedition financed and in preparation.

Immediately after the revolution I urged upon President Machado, who professed to have no further political ambitions, that he take advantage of his victory to enact drastic and liberal political reforms. I pointed out to him that although physical conflict had been halted, at least for the moment, there still remained the far more difficult task of establishing moral peace, without which Cuba in its state of economic, political and financial exhaustion could not recover. Because of his victory, he was in a position to impose his will on the politicians and bring about sweeping reforms that the awakened consciousness of the people was demanding and would acclaim. The essential formula, in my opinion, was nothing short of enacting sweeping constitutional reforms, including the modification of the Congressional immunity provision, the choice of a Vice-President by the Supreme Court with certain safeguards to prevent the appointment of a partisan, and the appointment of a Supreme Electoral Board with full powers to supervise elections. In order to restore confidence, the Vice-President should assume the presidency two months before the elections, or September 1, 1932. I told President Machado that unless some such program were carried out in good faith, there could be no moral peace in Cuba. Without moral peace, there could be no recovery from the economic, political and financial crisis. Without this recovery, the Government would inevitably collapse.

President Machado accepted the suggestion and actually sent a message to Congress asking for adequate legislation. But he had a change of heart, influenced by some of his advisers who assured him that he was under no compulsion to pass reforms. He permitted his message to die in the Congress.

On December 4, 1931, referring to this matter I said to President Machado: "The fundamental situation seems to be that the politicians want all or nothing; before the revolution, the oppositionists were unwilling to compromise—they wanted all and got nothing. Since the revolution, the Government politicians are determined to have all or nothing and it remains to be seen whether they will continue to have all or nothing." History has recorded the answer.

If we disregard those superficial differences of manners and customs that distinguish the man of Latin origin from the one of Anglo-Saxon origin, there remains aside from the different tempo in life a fundamental difference in the Cuban's and the North American's view of human relations. The North American believes in the theory of justice to the community as a whole. It often seems to the Cuban a cold and relentless justice. It is exemplified in the incident of the Teapot Dome investigation when Senator Thomas Walsh, the chief prosecutor, examined the oilman, Edward L. Doheny. They had been such close friends that on the death of his wife the Senator went to the home of the oilman for rest and consolation. They had a common birthplace, religion and political affiliation. Yet when the prosecutor was faced with the fulfillment of his public duty "seemingly unmindful of their long friendship, Walsh stared into the baby-blue eyes of the roly-poly prospector from across the committee table, and wrung from him a story, which, at the moment, seemed to point to jail and disgrace." [6] Such an act would be improbable in Cuba. The fact that "alone in his apartment, Walsh all but wept at the hurt he had been forced to give his former friend and host—Doheny" would not have excused in the Cuban eyes the Senator's "inhumanity".

It is that viewpoint in Cuba which requires a judicial system without trial by jury. There would be few verdicts of "guilty" by juries in Cuba. The Cuban demands a loyalty to family, friends, political and business associates, and friends of friends, that

[6] Ray Tucker, *Sons of the Wild Jackass*, Boston, pp. 126-127.

creates a human relationship quite distinct from that in America. The Anglo-Saxon tradition of "playing cricket" includes the personal sacrifice of one's son or one's best friend if he has violated the code.

In the Cuban eye such cold justice leads to an inhuman outlook and a barren, joyless, puritanical life. He believes that on its path is found the efficient, but sometimes cold hand of organized charity. In Cuba the hand has little to give, but the heart overflows with sympathy for one's own. There is little organized philanthropy, but no man need starve if his remote relative or friend has a meal to share with him, no matter how undeserving he may be. Perhaps the Cuban philosophy is destructive to the Anglo-Saxon foundation of social justice on which a great political and material progress has been built. But there is a warmth in the Cuban life that the Anglo-Saxon sometimes misses on his more austere march to progress.

· · · · ·

These political activities exemplify some of the differences in the temperament and psychology of the two peoples. In time, these differences, if mutually approached with patience and sympathy, will strengthen the contacts between the two nations and contribute to a richer philosophy in both countries. For the present, they constitute a barrier against popular understanding and unfortunately are cleverly

POLITICAL ACTIVITIES

utilized by the unscrupulous in both countries to further some special interest.

It is perhaps natural that the art of propaganda should be particularly well developed in a "country so small as Cuba, so incapable as she must always be, to contend by force against the great powers of the world". The systematic and subtle methods of the Cuban propagandist are extremely difficult for the uninitiated to fathom. The method is often so remote, the impression to be created of such slight importance that it seems incomprehensible that it can be part of a campaign. Yet through the deposit at one's doorstep of grain upon grain of propaganda by a persistent army of collaborators, there is gradually built up a mound across one's path that is at least arresting to the eye.

In this connection, it should be stated that the Cuban press lends itself to misinterpretations of this kind. In the United States we take it for granted that the press is independent, even though it may be biased and frequently sensational; that is, we know that American newspapers are neither subsidized nor censored by the Government, and that their news columns are not for sale. But outside of the United States and Great Britain, and a very few other countries we can by no means assume that this admirable condition always exists.

In Latin America, particularly, a great many newspapers are susceptible to Government pressure. Government censorship is almost always more or less of a factor in influencing the news; and conversely, when the censorship is entirely lifted, the newspapers tend to exhibit a degree of unrestraint which the term "freedom of the press" does not usually signify. Americans who are horrified to learn of the extent to which some Governments suppress or distort the news, would be equally horrified to learn of the extent to which the press, when temporarily freed from censorship, distorts its own news reports or indulges in personal attacks of a kind rare in our own country. As every American correspondent in Havana knows, a reporter's day in that city consists of a long effort in trying to find what fact, if any, lies at the bottom of rumors freely handed out by Government officials as well as private citizens.

Traditionally the Cuban inaugurates his propaganda campaign in the United States by establishing there a junta, or revolutionary committee. There are, as a rule, three points of concentration for the junta; one in New York where financial aid is solicited and filibustering expeditions are organized; one in Washington where political aid is sought; and one in Miami where the rank and file of émigrés and followers of the junta concentrate, since they can live more easily in Florida's sunshine. The usual activities consist in direct and indirect statements for the newspapers and magazines, enlisting the aid of Representatives and Senators (using the lure of publicity when

POLITICAL ACTIVITIES 177

the appeal to reason fails), the raising of funds by generous promises of rich rewards, and the enrollment in their cause of American citizens who for strange and disparate motives join their ranks. These Cuban opposition groups usually start with the advantage that in Cuban politics those out of office gain the sympathy of the American people because of the abuses of the officeholders.

As early as 1848 when Narciso López, the Cuban revolutionary fugitive, reached New York, he found Cuban juntas established in the United States. They were intermittently active during this initial period of revolution and during Cuba's ten years war from 1868 to 1878. Later the Cuban revolutionary party renewed its activity in New York in April, 1892, and "this New York Junta, meeting at 56 New Street, New York City, was the real head of the whole movement" [7]—the forerunner of the War of Independence.

Commenting on the junta and the Cuban insurgents, the Spanish Ambassador to Washington, Dupuy de Lôme, stated in a communication to the Foreign Relations Committee of the Senate:

"They know they cannot succeed, and their only hope is founded, directed by the Junta in New York, in what they most desire—on the possibility of bringing difficulties in the relations of Spain and the United States".[8]

[7] Willis F. Johnson, *op. cit.*, Vol. IV, p. 3.
[8] Walter Millis, *op. cit.*, p. 44.

When the Republic was finally established, the first President to be elected was don Tomás Estrada Palma, who had been President of the Junta in New York. The Secretary of the Junta became the first Minister to Washington, and its General Counsel, an American, became the head of vast commercial enterprises on the island after the founding of the Republic. This precedent for rewarding the juntas has induced many less worthy Cubans, at various times since then, to believe in the value of junta activities. Since the establishment of the Republic, there never has been a political controversy of importance in Cuba which was not accompanied by the traditional method of organizing a junta to involve the United States in the controversy.

The term junta connotes such dignity and importance, especially among a highly individualistic people like the Cubans, that some Cuban friends and I were amused to hear it used one day by some country boys in the shooting fields. We had been shooting, in the formidable Zapata Swamp, a difficult game bird called the *torcaza*, a species of white-headed wild pigeon. The guns were stationed along the high ground of a railroad track, and the birds crossed it at a great height flying from a roosting to a feeding ground. Each gun had with him a country lad who acted as a human retriever, and was dignified with the name of *secretario* or secretary. The boys were extraordinarily alert and active and rarely lost a bird,

POLITICAL ACTIVITIES 179

which was no mean achievement, not only because of the rocky and brush-covered terrain, but also because the country abounded with land crabs whose predatory instincts were so acute that they even carried off to their holes exploded cartridge shells. When a bird fell, there instantaneously began a race for possession between a *secretario* and innumerable land crabs. I wounded a bird which fell quite far off. My boy raced after it and didn't return with his usual promptness, but in the distance there arose a great chatter of youngsters. Finally my boy returned crestfallen. The bird had disappeared, probably down a land crab's hole, but the boy had only given up, as he expressed it, after he had exhausted every effort, even to the calling of a *junta de secretarios* to consider the question.

During the time that I was in Cuba juntas were active in the United States. Even before I left for my post, I was beset by junta members, some of whom were Cuban politicians in exile, while others were simply opportunists, attaching themselves for personal gain to what they hoped would be a successful cause. As our Government's policy of non-intervention in Cuban affairs did not favor their personal ambitions, they directed some of their energies to attacking the American Ambassador and sometimes the Secretary of State.

In this they made use of the activities of elements in the United States including: (1) Americans who were pressing unjust claims against Cuba to which the Department of State and the Embassy could not give their support; (2) some American reform groups which were outraged by the illiberality of the Machado régime and who accepted the entirely false statement of the Cuban propagandists that the Embassy was upholding the Machado Government; (3) a certain few American writers and "experts" in Latin America who are inclined to accept and reiterate, without scrutiny, any sensational attack upon United States policies or actions in Latin American countries.

When I assumed my post in Havana in 1929, a junta in the United States was busily engaged in bringing the Cuban question before the American people through what I have called the "claims racket". This racket consists in attempting to force the payment of an unjust or doubtful claim against the Cuban Government, or to procure prior or special consideration for a just claim in prejudice to the rights of other creditors. The technique of this racket is to intimidate and discredit both petty and major Cuban and American government officials through a campaign in the press and Congress of the United States.

The propaganda pictures a friendless American citizen in a foreign country, despoiled of his life's labor by a corrupt system of justice, abetted by a grafting, dictatorial executive, and ignored by the weak foreign representative of the American Govern-

POLITICAL ACTIVITIES 181

ment and a lethargic Department of State. There is always enough of historic reality in this picture to create a certain amount of sympathy for the "victim". This traffic in international discord is usually fostered by a combination of Americans and Cubans, at least technically citizens of their respective countries. Sometimes the claims racketeer is even subsidized to carry on his propaganda by the junta in the United States working for the overthrow of the Cuban Government and is promised immediate settlement of his claim as soon as the junta's party "gets in". The "claims racket" is not only a distinctly irritating factor in relations between the United States and Cuba, but in addition it prejudices the just claims which the Department of State is frequently called upon to press for its citizens.

Occasionally American business men resident in Cuba will establish privileged relations with a Cuban administration and then attempt to get the United States to support that administration. There is one especially interesting illustration of how an American capitalist tried to use our Government to strengthen the hand of President Machado, and thus promote his own special interest. In April, 1930, the *Unión Nacionalista*—at that time the only active political group opposed to President Machado—was organizing a great political rally, to meet in Havana. In an attempt to stamp out this political opposition, the President issued a decree prohibiting any meetings during the *zafra*, the sugar harvest. The Supreme Court declared the decree unconstitutional, and President Machado, who at that time was endeavoring to rule the country within Constitutional limits, revoked his decree. The meeting was then fixed for a date late in April, and it was anticipated that some ten to twenty thousand people would be present.

During this period I received a telegram from the Department of State informing me that two warships would pay a courtesy call at Havana harbor between certain dates at the end of April, but with the usual appended phrase "if you perceive no objection to this visit". I did not think it wise to have American warships in Havana harbor during the mass meeting for two reasons: first, I feared there might be rioting and bloodshed resulting from the meeting, since both Government and Oppositionist nerves were on edge, and it did not seem wise to run the risk of having American naval officers and sailors in Havana where they might be drawn into a minor or major incident which could lead to serious consequences for the United States. And second, the visit of American warships would mean an exchange of courtesies with Cuban Government officials which I feared might be abused by President Machado to indicate the support of the Cuban Government by the Government of the United States.

At this time, President Machado's American supporter, to whom I have referred, informed me that he knew of the intended visit of the American warships; he was happy that they were being sent as they would create good will between the two countries, and with the exchange of dinners between the commanding officer and President Machado (an unusual courtesy) would indeed cement existing friendships. Much to the American's surprise and great displeasure, I advised him that the warships' orders would be cancelled as the time for their visit was inopportune. I realized then that this proposed visit was not merely an innocent movement of ships. On the following day I called on President Machado to inform myself further regarding his part in this incident and to counteract any difficulties that the American, by his incursion in diplomacy, might make for me with the President.

As anticipated, President Machado knew all about the proposed visit of the ships, and he did everything in his power to persuade me to let them come. I told him that it would be contrary to the best interests of the United States to have warships in Havana harbor during the proposed political demonstration, and that the visit would be unwise. The ships did not come. The American had suggested the visit through minor officials in Washington, and the ships had been ordered to Havana quite innocently by those in authority in the Navy Department. The proposal attracted little official notice because our warships are frequently cruising about these waters and stopping for courtesy visits at Havana. In my last two years in Cuba I prevented the entry of American warships into Havana harbor, much to the disgust of some of my old comrades in the navy whose visits I personally would have enjoyed as much as they.

Secretary Frelinghuysen once clearly stated a principle that American citizens abroad might ponder well before attempting to involve their Government in the politics of a foreign power or in supporting doubtful claims on their behalf:

> "American citizenship is a great privilege not to be lightly put on or unworthily worn. Its assumption implies the promise and the obligation to observe our laws at home, and peaceably as good citizens to assist in maintaining our faith abroad without efforts to entangle us in internal troubles or civil discord with which we have not and do not wish to have anything to do. When an American citizen thus conducts himself, whether at home or abroad, he is entitled to the confidence of his government and active support of all its officials." [9]

In a period of stress, claims for injury to person and property, which are a regular part of the business of a foreign mission, tend to increase. By adjusting many of these, including some which had attained a particular notoriety over a number of years, the Embassy eliminated some of the sensational charges circulated by the propagandists. The latter continued

[9] U. S. *Foreign Relations*, 1883, pp. 233-234.

their attempts to involve the United States in the internal affairs of Cuba by arousing American public opinion on behalf of Cubans oppressed by their Government. In the fall of 1930, I recommended that the "hands-off" policy of the United States be clarified. Secretary Stimson issued a statement pointing out that the United States was observing the official Root interpretation of the Platt Amendment. The propaganda then found itself vulnerable and had to shift its direction. Since the United States was not going to intervene on the side of the opposition, the Embassy was at once accused of upholding Machado.

The most fantastic tales on all subjects are circulated in Havana; the Cubans describe them graphically by the word *bola*, which signifies a rumor in the shape of a ball rolling around the city for everybody's misinformation. The Cubans enjoy the *bola* which is usually at the expense of someone's character, but they have learned to discount it. When the same stories are retailed for publication in the United States, however, they shock an uninformed public opinion. For example, a *bola* to the effect that in a public speech President Machado had threatened "to drown the country in blood" if he were opposed, and that "the American Ambassador applauded heartily", was published as a fact in the United States.

In the winter of 1931 it was reported that I had advocated a $300,000,000 loan on behalf of the Cuban Government. The report was wholly false; in fact, I had indicated my unalterable opposition to any increase in Cuba's bonded debt; the Cuban Government (itself pleased at the report as indicating its good credit standing) finally had to deny it; but the opposition circulated it as evidence of the Embassy's partisan attitude. The repercussions of such a rumor are indicated by the fact that *The New York Times* even published a long article on the front page in regard to the loan; a member of the United States Congress, without the slightest basis of fact, denounced the loan in the House, stating: "We have an Ambassador in Cuba at this time who is representing these international financial houses, and has been negotiating the present $300,000,000 loan".

The difficulties of the American Ambassador's position in Cuba were discussed in a letter published in *The New York Times* by Jacob Billikopf who, as a member of the Committee on Cultural Relations with Latin America, visited Cuba in 1931. This writer said in part:

"The American Embassy in Havana, of course, receives the cross fire of propaganda from both sides. The government propaganda would make it appear that the Machado Administration is firmly buttressed by the support of the American Ambassador, which means the United States, and the consequent implication that its position is unshakable. The opposition, which is apparently too uncoördinated to threaten effectively the stability of the Machado Government, must find a scapegoat somewhere and justify to itself and its fol-

POLITICAL ACTIVITIES 187

lowing its inability to dislodge Machado. The Ambassador serves as a convenient scapegoat and the attempt to make him such gives play to the deep-seated sentiment in Cuba hostile to American influence."

The Embassy's impartiality in Cuban politics was amply demonstrated during the attempted revolution in August, 1931.

Opposition leaders nevertheless continued to beg privately for United States intervention while publicly repudiating it. Although the propaganda against the Embassy seemed to moderate in 1932, it revived at the end of the year with a change in the American administration in sight and with a series of murders on both sides in Cuba.

The assassinations that stirred the Opposition particularly were those of several students shot while "attempting to escape" under the notorious *ley de fuga*. Relatives and friends of those who were imprisoned called at the Embassy to state their fears for the lives of the prisoners. Officially the American Ambassador had no right to ask the Cuban Government to protect a Cuban citizen, but in the name of humanity I interceded personally time and again to request a fair trial for political prisoners arrested by the Government. A large number of Cubans were protected by this unofficial intercession, including most of the opposition leaders. The rescued Cubans, while privately grateful, were reluctant to admit this publicly because it interfered with the propaganda against the American Embassy. The only instance that received public comment was the only one in which this intercession failed. In this case one of the many Cuban American propaganda organizations promptly denounced the American Ambassador for having "guaranteed" the life of the prisoner and then having failed to fulfill the guarantee!

A number of opposition leaders acknowledged in writing these unofficial services in saving the lives of their friends and themselves. One such letter, typical of the rest, and mentioning some of the many individuals involved, is quoted herewith. It was written by Dr. Miguel Antonio Riva, Commodore of the Havana Yacht Club and opponent of President Machado, to his chief, Colonel Carlos Mendieta, high-minded leader of the *Unión Nacionalista,* and later Provisional President of Cuba:

"The American Ambassador Mr. Harry F. Guggenheim, has had to address the Government in person very many times, in behalf of relatives or friends of those whose lives were threatened, or who were in jail and in danger of being murdered, to take steps to save their lives. Among the persons in whose behalf the American Ambassador has interceded, the following may be cited, Senator Collazo; Commander Espinosa; students Ruben León and R. Escalona; young Butari, nephew of the policeman assassinated, of the same name and surname; Mrs. Mariana de la Torre, Viuda de Mendoza; the University Professors Doctors Costales and Cuervo Rubio; the student Ángel Álvárez, assassinated by the police five hours after —— had assured the American

POLITICAL ACTIVITIES 189

Ambassador that his life would be respected; and, during the last few days, Attorneys Martínez Saenz and Marril, of the firm which has been the legal representation of the National City Bank of New York; and the student Guillermo McKinley Cancio. These steps had to be taken by the American Ambassador extra-officially in character and in a personal manner, since, according to the interpretation which the American State Department gives at present to the Platt Amendment—Elihu Root's interpretation—he has no power to make them in the form of an official representation, and consequently, he cannot adopt any official attitude in case his request is not heeded, as occurred in the case of the young student Ángel Álvárez, which was fully reported by all the press of the United States."

One of the Cuban leaders who had special reason to know of intercessions to save him and various members of his family, nevertheless (on February 14, 1933), issued to *The New York Times* a statement from Miami criticizing the Embassy for its hostility and asserting:

"Representatives of all these countries [Latin-American] except the United States have indicated friendliness toward our movement. Every Embassy except that of the United States in Havana is sheltering political refugees. Although the American Embassy is the one to which Cubans should turn most readily for protection in such times as these, I do not know of one Cuban who has gone there. Surely, there is a reason for that."

The "reason for that", as this critic knew, was that the American Embassy could not offer such asylum to political refugees since the United States has consistently opposed that doctrine and would not sign the Pan-American Asylum Treaty of 1928, to which Mexico and some other Latin American countries are signatories. The statement moreover was inaccurate since only one foreign mission was sheltering political refugees at that time.

The propaganda during the Machado régime followed a definite course which can be traced as follows: first, there was an effort to induce American intervention by attempting to demonstrate, especially through the "claims racket", that the Machado Government was not affording adequate protection to American citizens; second, when the American policy of non-interference was proclaimed, the American Government and its Embassy were accused of supporting Machado—an effort which was accompanied by personal abuse against the Ambassador, and denunciation of American imperialism and intervention; third, when the agents of the opposition's reign of terror fell into Machado's hands, there was a rush to the American Embassy to appeal for the "intervention" of the American Ambassador on behalf of these individuals.

At least it can be said that this propaganda was not effective in its ultimate object, which was to rouse public opinion in the United States and actually provoke intervention; it succeeded to a degree, however, in stirring up international antagonism, particularly on account of the extraordinary conditions of poverty and political bitterness on the island at that time. The same type of propaganda, slightly varied to meet a changed situation, has been directed against my successors in Cuba. It is for this reason that the facts of that propaganda, from which the personal slander is omitted, are published here—not so much because of a desire to clarify the past as to prevent an effective recurrence of such propaganda in the future. The unthinking acceptance of these charges by Americans, the reiteration of them by the American press, only heighten the difficulties that harass the relations between Cuba and the United States.

PART V

Unsatisfactory Evolution of the Relationship under the Permanent Treaty

WHEN the United States military occupation of Cuba came to an end, the official relations between the two countries were governed by the Platt Amendment and later by the Permanent Treaty. The two articles of the Treaty that were most frequently applied in these relations were Article II which imposed an obligation on Cuba in regard to her finances, and Article III which recognized the right of the United States to intervene in Cuba.

Shortly after my appointment to Cuba I had an exhaustive compilation made of the applications of the Treaty in order to study the historical record of its consequences. From this study it was apparent that the United States had not been consistent in its applications of the Treaty and had not strictly adhered to the official interpretation of Article III, made by Secretary Root after conferring with the Committee of the Cuban Constitutional Assembly. Article III of the Treaty reads:

"III. That the Government of Cuba consents that the United States may exercise the right to intervene for the preservation of Cuban independence, the maintenance of a government adequate for the protection of life, property, and individual liberty, and for discharging the obligations with respect to Cuba imposed by the Treaty of Paris on the United States, now to be assumed and undertaken by the government of Cuba."

The Root interpretation was as follows:

"You are authorized to state officially that in the view of the President the intervention described in the third clause of the Platt Amendment is not synonymous with the intermeddling or interference with the affairs of the Cuban Government, but the formal action of the Government of the United States, based upon just and substantial grounds, for the preservation of Cuban independence, and the maintenance of a government adequate for the protection of life, property, and individual liberty, and adequate for discharging the obligations with respect to Cuba imposed by the Treaty of Paris on the United States." [1]

The first American Minister to Havana—H. G. Squiers—began by making very clear his special status as the diplomatic representative of the United States. He reported on May 26, 1904, that Secretary of State Zaldo was apparently jealous of his conferences with the President and had sent him a note that thereafter all such interviews must be arranged with

[1] Elihu Root, *op. cit.*, p. 188.

the Department of State and must be accompanied by a statement of the purpose of the interview:

> "I immediately called at the Foreign Office and very plainly told Mr. Zaldo that the rule proposed could not be accepted. That the position of the American Minister vis-à-vis the Cuban Government was quite different than that of the diplomatic representatives of any other country; that I am here on quite a different basis, as is well understood; that I could not accept for a moment of a rule which limits in the least or changes in the slightest degree the relations which have existed up to this time between the President and myself, and pointed out to him how very short sighted it was to raise any such question; that there was no necessity for it, and much more to the same effect."

Squiers' viewpoint seems to have encountered no explicit remonstrance from either Zaldo or President Palma. When he sought the personal opinion of Mr. Loomis in the Department of State on his action, Loomis expressed general agreement, but hoped there would be no need to press the point.

In July, 1905, however, the Cuban Congress officially indicated its dislike of the Permanent Treaty. The House of Representatives passed a bill authorizing the publication of ten thousand copies of the Cuban Constitution, but expressly provided that the Appendix, which contained the provisions of the Platt Amendment, was not to be printed. An amendment to insert the Permanent Treaty in place of the Appendix was similarly discarded by sixteen votes to fifteen. This was indicative of the attitude of the politicians then and thereafter. They sought popularity by denouncing the Platt Amendment and seldom ran the risk of voicing any expression of gratitude to the United States for its efforts on behalf of Cuba's independence.

The American diplomatic representative was speedily involved in Cuba's political controversies. In September, 1905, Squiers reported on Cuba's first general election which had just been concluded. President Palma told him that it had been conducted quietly, but the Liberals charged all manner of fraud and intimidation (a situation frequently duplicated in subsequent years). Gómez and Zayas, the Liberal candidates for President and Vice-President, who were demanding new elections, asked for and obtained an interview with Squiers. President Palma knew of it and complained rather bitterly. Squiers assured him that his only interest was in the peace and quiet of Cuba and that he had no political motives at all. He said that he could probably discourage the political opposition from starting a revolution and could thus help Palma. He also mentioned that if trouble came and Palma could not control the situation, he would have to cable Secretary Root to send warships to protect American lives and property.

Gómez and Zayas, however, expressed no revolutionary sentiments. The Minister lectured them on their patriotic duty to Cuba; told them the United

States had no interest in any particular candidate and was interested only in the preservation of peace and order. President Palma wanted a full report on the above interview, but Squiers did not feel at liberty to give it to him, merely summarizing his own observations. Gómez subsequently withdrew from the contest on the ground that fair elections were impossible, thus setting a precedent for the future.

Misinterpretation of Article III by citizens of the United States began as early as December, 1905. Some manufacturers in the United States complained of discrimination against American firms by the Cuban Government. They wrote to Senator Hopkins asking him to use his influence "in the effort to compel the Republic of Cuba to comply with the clearly expressed terms of the Platt Amendment". A copy of this letter was sent to the Legation with instructions to make appropriate representations. The Chargé enclosed a copy of the letter with his note to the Cuban Government. On February 12, 1906, Root, then Secretary of State, wrote him that "it is not expedient to transmit to the Cuban Government letters which contain such inadmissible propositions. . . ." The transmittal of the letter, he said, might be open to the misconstruction that the Chargé shared the views expressed in it. "You will expressly disavow the statements of this letter and convey to the Secretary of State your regret for the inadvertence by which it was communicated."

UNSATISFACTORY RELATIONSHIP 197

In the latter part of August, 1906, revolutionary activities broke out in Cuba which led to the armed intervention and second occupation of Cuba by the United States. This intervention took place at the request of the Cuban Government and was strictly in accordance with the Root interpretation of the Treaty.

The revolution spread rapidly, and as the Government found itself unable to control the situation, it sought assistance from the United States. Negotiations were conducted through Consul-General Frank Steinhart rather than through the American Chargé d'Affaires. Steinhart's first telegram to the Secretary of State was sent on September 8, 1906, and read as follows:

"The secretary of state of Cuba has requested me, in the name of President Palma, to ask President Roosevelt to send immediately two vessels—one to Havana, another to Cienfuegos. They must come at once. The government is unable to protect life and property. President Palma will convene Congress next Friday, and Congress will ask for our forcible intervention. It must be kept secret and confidential that Palma asked for vessels. No one here, except President, secretary of state, and myself knows about it. Very anxiously awaiting reply. Send answer to Steinhart, Consul-General." [2]

He telegraphed again on the 10th of September that the President was worried because no reply had been received and asked that war vessels be sent im-

[2] U. S. *Foreign Relations*, 1906, Part I, p. 473.

mediately. On the same day, Mr. Bacon, Acting Secretary of State, telegraphed Steinhart that two ships had been sent, but emphasized the hope that the Cubans would handle the situation themselves, stating:

". . . The President directs me to state that perhaps you do not yourself appreciate the reluctance with which this country would intervene. . . . It is of course a very serious thing to undertake forcible intervention, and before going into it we should have to be absolutely certain of the equities of the case and the needs of the situation. . . ." [3]

There followed further telegraphic correspondence between the Acting Secretary of State and Steinhart, in which the Acting Secretary stated that the President believed "actual immediate intervention to be out of the question". He wanted Steinhart's opinion as to whether or not it would be advisable to send an "emphatic warning" of the imminence of intervention "unless the people of Cuba, for the sake of their country, find some way to settle their difficulties, irrespective of personalities, cease their contentions, and live in peace". Steinhart was further instructed to urge Palma "to use in the most effective manner all the resources at his command to quell the revolt".

On September 12th Steinhart transmitted the text of a message from the Secretary of State of Cuba "in his own handwriting":

[3] *Ibid.*, p. 474.

UNSATISFACTORY RELATIONSHIP 199

"The rebellion has increased in the provinces of Santa Clara, Havana, and Pinar del Río, and the Cuban Government has no elements to contend it, to defend the towns and prevent the rebels from destroying property. President Estrada Palma asks for American intervention, and begs that President Roosevelt send to Havana with rapidity two or three thousand men to avoid any catastrophe in the capital. The intervention asked for should not be made public until the American troops are in Havana. The situation is grave and any delay may produce a massacre of citizens in Havana." [4]

On the 13th the Acting Secretary received the following from Steinhart:

"President Palma, the Republic of Cuba, through me officially asks for American intervention because he can not prevent rebels from entering cities and burning property.

"It is doubtful whether quorum when Congress assembles next Friday, tomorrow. President Palma has irrevocably resolved to resign and to deliver the government of Cuba to the representative whom the President of the United States will designate as soon as sufficient American troops are landed in Cuba. This act on the part of President Palma to save his country from complete anarchy, and imperative intervention come immediately. . . ." [5]

When the ships arrived, the American Chargé and Captain Colwell, in command, called on President Palma to ask if the Cuban Government would guarantee adequate protection to the lives and property

[4] *Ibid.*, p. 476.
[5] *Ibid.*, pp. 477-478.

of American citizens in Havana. When Palma replied in the negative, the Chargé cabled the Department:

". . . It has, therefore, been decided between Captain Colwell and myself to land a battalion of one hundred men with three field pieces to occupy a central position near the Plaza de Armas, covering the two main thoroughfares of the city, said force to be used only in case of disorders within the city menacing American citizens' lives and property." [6]

Before this telegram was received in Washington, but after it had been sent by the Chargé, the Department telegraphed that the war vessels sent to Cuban waters were under the orders of the President, who would determine when and how they should be used for the protection of American life and property. The President directed that while the Chargé might request asylum on board for Americans in case of danger, he should not under any circumstances request the landing of marines or any armed force except under orders from the Department of State.

The Chargé replied:

"On receipt of your confidential cable of this evening instructing me under no circumstances to request landing of any armed force, I immediately requested Captain Colwell, who had already landed a force, as per my cable of this afternoon, to withdraw it."

But on the 14th the Department telegraphed: "It is

[6] *Ibid.*, p. 478.

UNSATISFACTORY RELATIONSHIP

not clear whether or not a guard has been left at the legation. If not, you are authorized to request such a guard from the *Denver*." However, on the same day the following telegram was sent to the Chargé over the signature of Theodore Roosevelt in typical T. R. vein:

"You had no business to direct the landing of those troops without specific authority from here. They are not to be employed in keeping general order without our authority. Notify me immediately if they cannot be taken to the American legation with the field pieces and kept there. Scrupulous care is to be taken to avoid bloodshed. Remember that unless you are directed otherwise from here the forces are only to be used to protect American life and property."

In replying to this instruction the Chargé telegraphed that the entire force was being reëmbarked.

On September 14th Mr. Steinhart cabled as follows:

"President Palma has resolved not to continue at the head of the Government, and is ready to present his resignation even though the present disturbances should cease at once. The Vice President has resolved not to accept the office. Cabinet Ministers have declared that they will previously resign. Under these conditions it is impossible that Congress will meet, for the lack of a proper person to convoke same to designate a new President. The consequences will be absence of legal power and therefore the prevailing state of anarchy will continue unless the United States Government will adopt the measures necessary to avoid this danger."[7]

[7] *Ibid.*, p. 479.

Probably President Roosevelt had already determined on his course, for he wrote Acting Secretary Bacon from Oyster Bay on the same day:

"In view of the cables which have been received, making it evident that President Palma intends to resign at the earliest opportunity, and that the vice-president and cabinet seem resolved to avoid taking upon themselves the responsibilities of government, and in view of the repeated requests of President Palma for the landing of troops and intervention, it is evident that we must act at once in such a way as to protect American interests by fulfilling American obligations to Cuba. Moreover, under the circumstances it is also evident that the ordinary type of diplomatic communication would in this case accomplish no good purpose. The situation in the island seems to be one of impending chaos, with no real responsible head, and the inclosed letter to Minister Quesada, which will be communicated to our chargé d'affaires at Havana for transmission to President Palma and for publication in the Cuban press, seems to offer the best way of communicating, not merely with the supposed governmental authorities, but with the Cuban people." [8]

The letter referred to by President Roosevelt was delivered to Señor Quesada, Cuban Minister in Washington, and follows in major part:

". . . For seven years Cuba has been in a condition of profound peace and of steadily growing prosperity.

"For four years this peace and prosperity have obtained under her own independent government. Her peace, prosperity and independence are now menaced: for of all possi-

[8] *Ibid.*, p. 480.

ble evils that can befall Cuba the worst is the evil of anarchy, into which civil war and revolutionary disturbances will assuredly throw her. Whoever is responsible for armed revolt and outrage, whoever is responsible in any way for the condition of affairs that now obtains, is an enemy of Cuba; and doubly heavy is the responsibility of the man who, affecting to be the especial champion of Cuban independence, takes any step which will jeopardize that independence. For there is just one way in which Cuban independence can be jeopardized, and that is for the Cuban people to show their inability to continue in their path of peaceful and orderly progress.

"This nation asks nothing of Cuba, save that it shall continue to develop as it has developed during these past seven years; that it shall know and practice the orderly liberty which will assuredly bring an ever increasing measure of peace and prosperity to the beautiful Queen of the Antilles. Our intervention in Cuban affairs will only come if Cuba herself shows that she has fallen into the insurrectionary habit, that she lacks the self-restraint necessary to secure peaceful self-government, and that her contending factions have plunged the country into anarchy. . . .

"Under the treaty with your Government, I, as President of the United States, have a duty in this matter which I cannot shirk. The third article of that treaty explicitly confers upon the United States the right to intervene for the maintenance in Cuba of a government adequate for the protection of life, property, and individual liberty.

"The treaty conferring this right is the supreme law of the land and furnishes me with the right and the means of fulfilling the obligation that I am under to protect American interests.

"The information at hand shows that the social bonds throughout the island have been so relaxed that life, property, and individual liberty are no longer safe. I have received authentic information of injury to, and destruction of, American property. It is in my judgment imperative for the sake of Cuba that there shall be an immediate cessation of hostilities and some arrangement which will secure the permanent pacification of the island.

"I am sending to Havana the Secretary of War, Mr. Taft, and the Assistant Secretary of State, Mr. Bacon, as the special representatives of this Government, who will render such aid as is possible toward these ends. I had hoped that Mr. Root, the Secretary of State, could have stopped in Havana on his return from South America, but the seeming imminence of the crisis forbids further delay. . . ." [9]

Secretary of War Taft and Mr. Bacon, accompanied by Mr. Morgan, the American Minister, arrived at Havana on board the *Des Moines* on September 19th and immediately began interviewing the members of the Government and leaders of the revolutionary party. They further discussed the situation with all types of persons from many parts of the island. On September 28th, President Palma convened Congress and submitted to it his resignation. Accordingly, on September 29th, Mr. Taft issued a proclamation which reads in part as follows:

"To the people of Cuba: The failure of Congress to act on the irrevocable resignation of the President of the Republic of Cuba, or to elect a successor, leaves this country without a government at a time when great disorder prevails, and requires that pursuant to a request of President Palma, the

[9] *Ibid.*, pp. 480-481.

necessary steps be taken in the name and by the authority of the President of the United States to restore order, protect life and property in the island of Cuba and islands and keys adjacent thereto, and for this purpose, to establish therein a provisional government.

"The provisional government hereby established by direction and in the name of the President of the United States will be maintained only long enough to restore order and peace and public confidence, and then to hold such elections as may be necessary to determine those persons upon whom the permanent government of the Republic should be devolved.

"In so far as is consistent with the nature of a provisional government established under authority of the United States, this will be a Cuban government conforming, as far as may be, to the constitution of Cuba. The Cuban flag will be hoisted as usual over the government buildings of the island. All the executive departments and the provincial and municipal governments, including that of the city of Havana, will continue to be administered as under the Cuban Republic. The courts will continue to administer justice, and all laws not in their nature inapplicable by reason of the temporary and emergent character of the Government will be in force." ... [10]

There can be little doubt on the face of the record that the United States intervened on this occasion with the greatest reluctance and with the greatest justification. Here was just such a condition of anarchy as Article III was designed to cover. Moreover, the intervention was expressly and spontaneously re-

[10] *Ibid.*, p. 491.

quested by the President of Cuba. Quesada recognized the fairness of the United States Government in a letter to Root on October 3rd, acceding to the latter's request that he should retain his post as Cuban Minister to Washington.

"I never doubted for an instant," he wrote, "as you have so timely said, that under the Cuban constitution and under the treaty by virtue of which the United States is now acting, you intervene but for the 'preservation of Cuban independence'. I am convinced that the American people are not covetous of us; only feel sympathetic concern in our sufferings and are not anxious for our downfall. I, as well as my people, trust the American administration in this sad hour of Cuba's history. I am convinced that the United States will do what is right by Cuba." [11]

On October 13, 1906, Charles Edward Magoon became provisional governor. He issued a proclamation stating that as soon as might be practicable, he would bring about "the restoration of the ordinary agencies and methods of government under the ... Cuban Constitution." His administration was extremely unpopular. The Cubans accused him bitterly of graft and corruption, and while those most familiar with his character and his work completely exonerate him from that charge, he apparently lacked the skill and fibre required of those who attempt the thankless task of settling the family troubles of Cuba.

[11] *Ibid.*, p. 488.

UNSATISFACTORY RELATIONSHIP 207

At least the American Provisional Government held to the principles established by President Roosevelt that the intervention was solely for the purpose of restoring an independent Government in Cuba. Its only desire was to hold an honest election as soon as possible and turn the country back to the Cubans.

Such a program was far more difficult than it might appear on the surface. The date for elections was postponed on several occasions until adequate preparations could be made for them. Magoon appointed an "Advisory Law Commission" consisting of nine Cubans and three Americans, presided over by Colonel Enoch Crowder, later to serve both America and Cuba so well as Special Representative and then Ambassador of the United States in Cuba. The task of this Commission included the preparation of an electoral code, laws for the provinces, municipalities, and judiciary and the civil service.

On November 14, 1908, José Miguel Gómez was elected President of the Republic under an election that was generally conceded to have been fairly conducted. On January 28, 1909, Magoon terminated his Governorship, thus holding steadily to the terms under which the intervention had been initiated.

. . . . .

In the years following 1909, however, the American Government's policy towards Cuba did not adhere so strictly to the terms of the Platt Amendment.

Our relations with Cuba are always subject to the varying political philosophies of changing American Government administrations. This results in a lack of consistency which is one of the greatest weaknesses in our foreign relations, as it hinders the effectiveness of any policy. The policy of Secretary of State Knox, 1909–1913, as contrasted with that of Hay and Root, was much more vigorous and assertive, not only in regard to Cuba, but to American interests throughout Central America and the Caribbean area. Although Bryan, on the other hand, was inclined to deal more gently with the Cuban situation, this policy generally prevailed until about 1925.

The departures from the Root interpretation of the Platt Amendment in this period are numerous. They affected, in particular, Articles II and III.

In the spring of 1911 Secretary Knox sent an instruction to the Legation at Havana regarding the lease of certain waterworks to private enterprise. In this instruction the Secretary forged a link between Articles II and III of the Permanent Treaty, stating the belief of the United States:

". . . . that it would indeed be remiss in its duty did it not formally and energetically bring to the attention of the Government of Cuba a state of affairs which it is believed if permitted to continue will ultimately bring the Republic of Cuba into a state of national bankruptcy; and there can be no doubt that a bankrupt government is not a government adequate for the proection of life, property, and individual

UNSATISFACTORY RELATIONSHIP

liberty within the meaning of Article III of the Treaty. Extravagant and improvident action by the Executive and Legislature of Cuba can as well bring that Government into a position where it will be no longer capable of discharging its international obligations as could possibly result from any domestic or foreign complications. . . ."

That this general point of view was not accepted by the Cuban Government was clearly pointed out in the Cuban Minister's note of August 11, 1911. The note is so typical an expression of the Cuban point of view that I quote from it at length:

"The President recommends me to call your attention to the fact that if the idea of the American Government [is] to consider itself, on account of the very interesting and glorious part taken by the United States in the preparation and advent of our independence, as holding some right to exercise over us some sort of moral action from a distance, with the generous purpose of helping us out of the difficulties which naturally arise in the course of the development of new nations, its exaggeration produces deplorable effects on the conscience of the country, on the exercise of the home government and even on the moral and economical life of the Nation, in that it gives birth, together with the belief that the fate of any government depends upon the will of the foreigner, to the disastrous principle that its own existence is essentially precarious, thus opening the way for the intrigues of the speculators and of the ambitious lacking in scruples, imbuing the public mind with reasons or tendencies to look upon the overthrow of established rule as a very easy undertaking, exalting social indiscipline and placing every government in the most delicate and dangerous condition before the machination, and irreverence that find support in their reliance upon the press or intrigue always to be an echo or facilitate the success of malice, error and calumny."

Secretary Knox, however, definitely espoused the theory of "preventive intervention."

On the basis of this theory, he attempted to forestall a threatened revolutionary outbreak in Cuba by the following note of January 16, 1912, which was transmitted to President Gómez and made public:

"The situation in Cuba as now reported causes grave concern to the Government of the United States.

"That the laws intended to safeguard free republican government shall be enforced and not defied is obviously essential to the maintenance of the law, order, and stability indispensable to the status of the Republic of Cuba, in the continued well-being of which the United States has always evinced and cannot escape a vital interest.

"The President of the United States therefore looks to the President and Government of Cuba to prevent a threatened situation which would compel the Government of the United States, much against its desires, to consider what measures it must take in pursuance of the obligation of its relations to Cuba." [12]

Minister Beaupre reported that this note "undoubtedly prevented a revolution in Cuba; and in view of the splendid results of this preventive measure, I venture to submit that similar action appropriately adapted to peculiar circumstances, would

[12] U. S. *Foreign Relations*, 1912, pp. 240-241.

have a like salutary effect" in the pending discussion of the Cuban electoral law.

President Gómez's note in July, 1912, written in response to a protest against the granting of the notorious concession for reclaiming the Zapata Swamp, vigorously objected to the policy of "meddling in internal affairs." He declared that he would not allow the independence of Cuba to be prejudiced by such "tutelage."

In the spring of 1912, Secretary Knox at first took no vigorous steps to head off a negro revolution. By the end of May, however, the Cuban Government was evidently unable to suppress sporadic violence, and naval vessels were sent to Cuban ports to protect American lives and property. Secretary Knox emphasized that "This is not intervention." President Gómez was not convinced, but an exchange of letters with President Taft served to clear the issue, at least for the moment. The point of view of Gómez, however, is a natural one for the Cuban to take; against the background of the Platt Amendment and the history of its application, legal distinctions between intervention and diplomatic protection are not always convincing.

Secretary Bryan, in general, did not follow closely the policy of his predecessor, Secretary Knox, but he seems to have acquiesced in a suggestion from our Minister that the marines who had been landed at Guantánamo during the negro revolution should not be withdrawn at the time lest the "significance of their withdrawal" be "distorted by certain elements into an evidence that the Government of the United States is now prepared to observe an absolute hands-off policy as regards revolution."

Secretary Lansing, however, seems to have returned to the Knox policy when in 1917 he effectually checked a revolt in Cuba by announcing that the United States would be hostile to it. On February 18, 1917, he cabled a statement for communication to the Cuban Government and for publication, in which he stated:

"One: The Government of the United States supports and sustains the Constitutional Government of the Republic of Cuba.

"Two: The armed revolt against the Constitutional Government of Cuba is considered by the Government of the United States as a lawless and unconstitutional act and will not be countenanced." [13]

On March 23, 1917, he emphasized this attitude in a second statement, which would be similarly disqualified by the Root interpretation of the Treaty:

"1. The Constitutional Government of Cuba has been and is being supported by the Government of the United States in the endeavor to restore order throughout the Republic.

"2. The Government of the United States, in emphasiz-

[13] U. S. *Foreign Relations*, 1917, p. 363.

UNSATISFACTORY RELATIONSHIP 213

ing its condemnation of the reprehensible conduct of those in revolt against the Constitutional Government in attempting to settle by force of arms disputes for which adequate legal remedies are provided, desires to point out that until those in revolt recognize their obligations as citizens of Cuba, have laid aside their arms and returned to their allegiance to the Constitutional Government, the United States cannot hold communication with any of them and will be forced to regard them as outside the law and beyond its consideration." [14]

On August 25, 1920, Secretary Colby attempted to prevent another imminent revolt in the same way. The phrase which I have italicized would imply that the treaty imposes obligations on the part of the United States under Article III:

"The Government of the United States does not propose actually to supervise the elections. However, *it is by treaty pledged* to 'the maintenance of a government in Cuba adequate for the protection of life, property and individual liberty'. It is, therefore, unalterably opposed to any attempt to substitute violence and revolution for the processes of government. I am desired to emphasize the fact, however, that it is no less opposed to intimidation and fraud in the conduct of elections as such procedure might be effective in depriving the people of Cuba of their right to choose their own government."

On January 1, 1921 General E. H. Crowder proceeded to Cuba on a United States cruiser to undertake a special mission as personal representative of

[14] *Ibid.*, pp. 387-388.

the President. In the following April Secretary Hughes instructed him:

"Doctor Zayas should be advised at the outset that the government of the United States believes that there is implicit in the treaty of 1903 the obligation on the part of the Republic of Cuba to maintain an honest and efficient government in return for the obligations assumed by the United States. Doctor Zayas, this government believes, will readily agree that his administration will not be able to maintain the high standards of efficiency and integrity which this Government realizes it is his earnest desire to have it maintain, unless his appointees to Cabinet positions are men of the highest ability and unquestioned honesty."

In March, 1922, General Crowder, with the approval of Secretary Hughes, began to send his now famous series of fifteen memoranda to Zayas, making explicit and detailed recommendations as to how the government should be conducted. In the third of these memoranda he said:

"I need not remind Your Excellency with what you are historically familiar, namely, that the interest of my Government in the framing of the Constitution of Cuba was not confined to those parts of it which fix Cuba's relationship to the United States, but extended to each and every provision whose authority could be invoked in the maintenance of a Government adequate for the protection of life, property and individual liberty, and for the discharge of the obligations devolving upon the United States under the Treaty of Paris. The reading of Mr. Root's letter of February 9,

1901, and related documents, some of which he cites, makes this abundantly plain. My Government has, of course, the same interest in any amendments thereto which might infringe the limitations and safeguards which the experience of Constitutional Government has shown to be necessary to the maintenance of orderly and stable Government."

The above illustrations refer to the broad interpretation given to Article III following the American Provisional Government.

. . . . .

Article II, which deals with the contracting of loans, is of far easier interpretation than the political article, but its application has been similarly altered to suit different administrations in the United States and Cuba. The article provides:

"The Government of Cuba shall not assume or contract any public debt to pay the interest upon which and to make reasonable sinking fund provision for the ultimate discharge of which, the ordinary revenues of the Island of Cuba, after defraying the current expenses of Government, shall be inadequate."

The original purpose of Article II was stated by Mr. Root in his letter of February 9, 1901, to General Wood, when he said:

"The preservation of that independence by a country so small as Cuba, so incapable, as she must always be, to contend by force against the great powers of the world, must depend upon her strict performance of international obligations, upon her giving due protection to the lives and property of the citizens of all other countries within her borders, and upon her never contracting any public debt which in the hands of citizens of foreign powers shall constitute an obligation she is unable to meet." [15]

While this provision of the treaty seems to have been designed originally to prevent a European creditor from having an occasion to impair the independence of Cuba by forcible collection of unpaid loans, it has, in subsequent practice, acquired a broader significance. The Cuban Government has never incurred a direct financial obligation to any but American bankers, and the danger of European aggression has never been imminent in this connection. But the general interest of the United States in the welfare and independence of Cuba has induced a careful attention to all the public debts incurred by the Cuban Government, and all such debts are included within the letter of the treaty.

The first foreign loan of the Cuban Government was not floated until 1904, but the relation of the Platt Amendment to such loans was discussed at an earlier period. As early as July, 1902, before ratification of the Treaty, Minister Squiers discussed this question with President Estrada Palma. Proposals for a loan were already being considered in Cuban circles, and the matter was brought up by the Minis-

---

[15] Elihu Root, *op. cit.*, p. 210.

ter in his weekly conferences with the President. His report of the conversation, which was acknowledged by Secretary Hay without comment, was as follows:

"I mentioned the provisions of the Platt Amendment regarding loans and inquired whether he understood that Cuba could make a loan without reference to the United States as to whether such provision had been complied with, and he replied that in his opinion no such reference was necessary." . . .

The Department did not comment then or later when advised that the law approving the loan of $35,000,000 had been passed by the Congress.

In July, 1903, President Palma suggested in a message to Congress, that a commission visit the United States and Europe for the purpose of getting the best possible terms for the loan; he expressed some doubt as to the possibility of floating it in the United States. To the Minister he indicated the probability that it would be floated in London or Paris. It is not clear whether this move was induced by a desire to demonstrate Cuban independence of the United States or whether it was felt that a gesture toward Europe would induce the Department of State to take steps to facilitate a loan in New York. The Commission sailed for New York in September, 1903, and in February, 1904, the contract was signed with an American firm. The Legation made no official representations as to the Platt Amendment and sought no information as to the condition of Cuban governmental finances.

In response to an inquiry from the bankers, the Department of State wrote them on February 27, 1904, that "this Government does not consider that there is occasion to object to such issue of bonds by reason of Article II of the appendix to the Constitution of Cuba, adopted pursuant to the requirements of the so-called Platt Amendment".

On November 23, 1904, Hay wrote a personal letter to Squiers, in which his attitude and that of President Roosevelt are defined; the postscript is especially interesting. The letter follows:

"My dear Mr. Squiers:
"We hear every day renewed stories of the pressure that is brought to bear from interested quarters upon President Palma to embark on an indefinite current of borrowing and pledging the resources of Cuba for all sorts of purposes. The clamor of the old soldiers, which is reinforced by a strong lobby of brokers in New York, the attempt of railroad companies to induce the Government to guarantee the payment of large sums on their securities, and various other incidents of the same sort have caused a good deal of anxiety in the mind of the President in regard to the future solvency of the Republic of Cuba. He does not wish you to assume the attitude of taking charge of the financial system of the Republic, but he desires that *you shall at all times, in a discreet and friendly manner, impress upon the mind of* President Palma and the Cuban Government the disastrous consequences of this wasteful and thoughtless policy. It seems to

UNSATISFACTORY RELATIONSHIP 219

us that the Government of Cuba is passing through a critical stage; that unless these extravagant schemes meet with some check, a great financial disaster is not far distant.

"I know in writing you this I am placing upon you a great responsibility, as it will require the exercise of extreme discretion, while impressing the President with the gravity of the situation not to assume an attitude of dictation, or even intermeddling, but I trust you will see the situation in its true light and be able to carry out the wishes of the President with tact and judgment.

"Very sincerely yours,
JOHN HAY.

"P.S. The President is very reluctant to avail himself of the provisions of the Platt Amendment in this and similar cases, but you will understand that this will become imperative unless the present dangerous tendency is checked."

In April, 1909, Minister Morgan reported to Secretary Knox on a proposed deal between the Cuban Government and the United Railways for an exchange of lands on the harbor front and the erection of public buildings involving a financial obligation of the Cuban Government. Mr. Morgan stated various objections to the Department of State in regard to this transaction. In reply he received the following instruction, quoted in part:

"Should the loan proposed be found to be practically imminent, you may make very clear to the Cuban authorities, to the United Railways of Havana, and to your British colleague the meaning which this Government attaches to Article 2 of the Appendix to the Cuban Constitution.

"It will also be entirely proper for you, in your discretion, to make friendly and appropriate use of your Legation's influence, with a view to discourage any exchange of property which may be very unwise, not only as a bad bargain, but also by depriving the Cuban Government of a water front property which may, in the future, become of important value to it."

One of the notorious scandals in the early history of the Cuban Republic was the Ports Company project which became the object of several invocations of Article II of the Permanent Treaty. The project was a scheme for the dredging and improving of certain harbors in Cuba to be financed by a public flotation made attractive by a concession to the Ports Company from the Cuban Government. The concession, involving both Cubans and Americans, provided for an impost over a long period of time on all goods imported through the new ports. The financing was arranged by Americans, but the issuing house was an English banking concern which inquired of the United States Government whether any objection would be raised to the flotation of $10,000,000 of bonds of the Cuban Ports Company. On June 9, 1911, the Department of State informed the bankers that careful examination had convinced the Department:

"That the contract is on its face so manifestly improvident and one-sided, that it so lacks in equity and reasonableness, that it imposes such burdensome and excessive taxes on Cuban commerce, and that it so vitally affects the ordinary

UNSATISFACTORY RELATIONSHIP

revenues of Cuba which were already scarcely adequate to defray the expenses of the Government, as to raise grave doubts regarding its ultimate validity and legality."

The English bankers replied that they hoped that no adverse opinion or influences would be permitted to prejudice the security of the bondholders. The Department commented that it would seem "that the promoters now have ample opportunity to put the bondholders in *statu quo ante* should they so choose". Minister Jackson informed the Department on July 14, 1911, that a copy of the Department's letter to the London bankers had circulated in Havana and had "caused a considerable amount of excitement and irritation".

On June 5, 1912, the American Minister was instructed to send a note to the Cuban Secretary of State. This note stated that "after a careful examination of the subject, the Government of the United States has reached the conclusion that this concession as it stands at present does not strictly conform to the requirements of Article II of the Appendix to the Constitution of Cuba, which also constitutes Article II of the treaty of May 22, 1903, between the United States and Cuba".

Secretary Knox continued by stating that the United States Government was aware that the constitutionality of the concession had been unsuccessfully challenged in the Cuban Courts, but he remarked that the question of its bearing upon Article II of the Treaty had not and could not be the subject of conclusive determination by the Courts of Cuba. He quoted Article II of the Treaty and stated that the provision for setting aside specific revenue for the remuneration of the Ports Company:

"may fairly be regarded as equivalent to payment of interest on the obligation and to making reasonable sinking fund provision for its discharge as contemplated in Article II aforesaid. But it will be noted that under the provisions of that Article this is permissible only if the ordinary revenues of the island are adequate for that purpose after first defraying the current expenses of government. The revenues from the tonnage tax which are to be devoted to paying the obligation under this concession are clearly ordinary revenues of the island within the meaning of Article II, but in order to meet this obligation the concession requires that the entire revenues so derived, whatever they amount to, must be paid over to the Cuban Ports Company. No deduction from such revenues is permissible for any purpose under the terms of the concession, which expressly provides that they must be 'turned over to it weekly in full, without deductions on any account'.

"For the reasons above set forth, it is evident that if at any time during the next thirty years, the ordinary revenues of the island, which under this concession are diverted to another purpose, should be required to defray the current expenses of government, the question of the validity of this concession will necessarily be forced upon the attention of this Government. It seems appropriate, therefore, that the Cuban Government, on account of its concern in the question of the ultimate validity of this concession, should be in-

UNSATISFACTORY RELATIONSHIP 223

formed in advance that the Government of the United States regards as objectionable, under the provisions of Article II, the requirements of the concession that a specified portion of the ordinary revenues, derived from the import tonnage tax, be paid over to the Cuban Ports Company regardless of whether or not such revenues are necessary to defray the current expenses of government, and that the Government of the United States reserves the right to insist upon this objection whenever in its judgment appropriate occasion shall arise."

It will be noted that this project did not involve the assumption of a "public debt" by the Cuban Government, but merely a pledging of future revenues. The concession was finally cancelled and a settlement made with the company's innocent bondholders and stockholders who had been the victims of the promoters and the Cuban politicians.

On November 21, 1913, Secretary Bryan instructed Minister González regarding his view of a controversy between two American banking houses over alleged preferential features in contracts made by the Cuban Government with the two houses. The Minister was instructed to inform the Cuban Government that such clauses, granting preferential rights, "have a tendency to restrict competition and therefore embarrass the Government of Cuba in the securing of money." Mr. Bryan continued:

"You may say to the Foreign Office therefore that, if they desire the opinion of this Government, they are advised against the incorporation of these or similar provisions in future contracts. They need not be assured that our only purpose in expressing an opinion is to aid them in securing money on the lowest terms. It is the policy of this Government to treat all Americans alike and to give all an equal opportunity insofar as the influence of this Government goes; but in advising the Latin American states it is our desire to look at the question from their standpoint and to give them every assistance that we properly can to the end that they may make the most of their opportunities and secure for their people the largest advantages obtainable."

In July, 1917, President Menocal asked and received from the Cuban Congress authority for a thirty million dollar loan. The Department had not previously been consulted about such a loan and promptly instructed the Minister, on July 19th, to remind the Cuban Government of the treaty provisions as to loans and the previous practice of "submitting full data as to existing and proposed new indebtedness and revenues applicable to payment of principal and interest."

In 1920 Cuba suffered a major financial crisis. The need of the Cuban Government at this time for the assistance of American bankers in finding a solution for their difficulties made it easier for General Crowder to exact compliance with his demands in regard to projected loans.

On February 11, 1921, the Department telegraphed the Legation that it understood that President Menocal had submitted to Congress a budget of some seventy millions more than that of 1918–1919. The Legation was instructed by Mr. Colby to bring to the attention of the President "the very grave anxiety which this action . . . is causing the Government of the United States." The Legation was authorized to act with General Crowder in taking such steps as might be necessary to prevent the enactment of the proposed budget. Conversations apparently ensued, and the President gave assurance that no effort would be made to pass the new budget.

The broad view taken by Secretary Hughes of Article II of the Platt Amendment is indicated in his telegram of June 17, 1921, to General Crowder in which he stated:

"Since the financial rehabilitation of Cuba in the opinion of the Department, affects very directly the stability of the Government in Cuba which it is the obligation of the United States under the Treaty of 1903 to maintain President Zayas will doubtless appreciate the reasons for the special interest which this phase of the situation in Cuba causes this Government."

On July 31, 1921, General Crowder sent a despatch to the Secretary of State in which he reviewed the provisions of Article II of the Permanent Treaty and discussed their application. He called attention to the fact that the treaty provision was a constitutional limitation upon the Cuban Government's borrowing capacity. He believed that the public debts of the provinces and the municipalities were also within the terms of the article.

In a letter of August 22, 1921, to Secretary Hughes, General Crowder urged that his policy of offering advice to President Zayas should be strengthened, stating:

"I am firmly of the opinion that the procedure that we have followed thus far of attempting to accomplish our program by advice to the Zayas administration, though disappointing to me in the actual results obtained, has won for us this distinct advantage. It has demonstrated even to the Cuban people the necessity and justification for a firmer attitude by our Government."

On February 9, 1922, General Crowder sent a note to President Zayas stating that "the Government of the United States is entitled to know, in the case of any public debt contemplated by the Government of Cuba, what 'the ordinary revenues' are, from what sources they are derived, and what said sources have produced and may be expected to produce." Attention was then directed to the existing financial difficulties of the Government which involved a failure to meet current obligations and were said to constitute such a condition of affairs as infringed Article II of the Permanent Treaty.

In his reply of February 21, President Zayas said that he had not doubted the friendly feeling of the

United States Government, and he expressed appreciation of General Crowder's services. In discussing the interpretation of Article II of the Permanent Treaty, President Zayas enunciated the following views:

"In regard to these rights, I agree that Cuba, on obligating itself under Article II of the Permanent Treaty with the United States not to assume or contract any public debt unless relying upon adequate ordinary revenues for the payment of interest and amortization, after covering its current expenses, recognizes that the Government of the United States is authorized to judge whether such condition is filled; and this authority implies that of requesting and examining data on which to base judgment. . . .

"Although from these articles of the Permanent Treaty there is not derived the right of the United States to inform itself regarding the maintaining of the ordinary revenues, and their relation to the expenditures, it is possible to admit that for the purpose of assuming or contracting a new public debt, it is essential to know and to study this point.

"I differ somewhat from your Excellency's opinion, when your Excellency states that a situation infringing Article II of the Permanent Treaty is created by the fact that the Treasury of Cuba owes sums under various heads to employees, private individuals, and organizations. What this article prohibits is the assuming or contracting of a public debt without fulfilling certain requisites, and as long as the Government does not try to convert into public debt the indebtedness to certain private entities, or does not try to contract a loan for payment thereof, the occasion does not exist for invoking Article II of the aforesaid Treaty."

A $50,000,000 loan was brought out by an American banking house in January, 1923. It is interesting to note that the public circular advertising the loan bears at the top this note:

"Issued with the acquiescence of the United States Government under the provisions of the Treaty dated May 22, 1903."

In the body of the notice there is a paragraph entitled "Agreement with the United States", under which the terms of the first three articles of the Platt Amendment are summarized. The loan contract recites:

"That the ordinary revenues of the Republic, after defraying the current expenses of the Government, are more than adequate to pay the interest upon, and to make reasonable sinking fund provision for the ultimate discharge of, the public debt which is the subject of this deed, all within the meaning and purpose of Article II of the Permanent Treaty between the Republic and the United States of America, and the Government of the United States of America, being advised in the premises, has formally acquiesced in the creation of such public debt."

The advertisement accompanying the circular, contains an interesting comment on Cuban relations with the United States as follows:

"There are three very important factors on which the credit of the Republic of Cuba is based. One is its ability to contribute to the world a large proportion of a basic product so essential as sugar; another is its proximity to the United States, its principal market; the third is the special interest which the United States has taken in the maintenance of peace and prosperity in the Island of Cuba, as evidenced by both treaty and precedent. . . .

"Through General E. H. Crowder, the personal representative of the President of the United States, who is acting under the direction of Secretary Hughes and in cordial coöperation with President Zayas, economies in governmental operations and increases in governmental revenues have been brought about, the result in the first six months of the present fiscal year being a surplus of income over expenses of approximately $1,000,000."

These illustrations are sufficient to indicate the important and varying powers which the United States appears to have assumed under the Permanent Treaty, beyond the official Root interpretation.

There has been a *laissez faire* policy and a tutorial policy; there have been lectures, admonitions, and threats; there has been a policy based on a strict construction of the Platt Amendment, and a policy based on a broad construction.

As pointed out, the Cuban Government did not accept these variations without protest. On June 20, 1922, the Cuban Senate protested against the Crowder policy in the following resolution, in part:

"When the Platt Amendment was considered by the Cuban Constituent Assembly, it was accepted in the light of the interpretation which the Military Governor of the

Island, in the name of the President of the United States, gave in his letter of April 2, 1901, i.e., that it was not synonymous with interference or intervention in the affairs of the Cuban Government.

"The Senate declares that the people of Cuba desires that the action of the United States Government in our domestic affairs conform to the spirit and the letter of the Platt Amendment, as it was set forth in the interpretation above referred to."

In 1927 when the Pan-American Federation of Labor protested against labor conditions in Cuba, the Cuban Ambassador, Dr. Orestes Ferrara, declared in regard to the Platt Amendment:

"I do not understand . . . that there is any authority, no matter how high, that will have any right to judge our internal actions . . . We believe that we are the only judges of our internal acts . . ."

. . . . .

In view of this confusion it seemed desirable to obtain a clarification of the policy that would govern my acts as Ambassador to Cuba, after my appointment in the fall of 1929. In September, 1930, therefore, I asked Secretary of State Stimson for a declaration of policy for my guidance. As stated at that time, it seemed to me that there were two considerations which must determine the relations between the two governments:

First, recognizing Cuba as an independent state, the United States was bound to observe the rules of international law governing the relations between states.

Second, the United States was bound to observe the terms of its Permanent Treaty with Cuba.

I stated:

"So far as I have been able to ascertain, the authoritative interpretation of Article III of the Platt Amendment and of the Permanent Treaty, in which the terms of this article are incorporated, is that expressed, under authority of President McKinley, in Secretary Root's telegram to General Wood, of April 3, 1901. This telegram reads as follows:

" 'You are authorized to state officially that in the view of the President, the intervention described in the third clause of the Platt Amendment is not synonymous with the intermeddling or interference with the affairs of the Cuban Government, but the formal action of the Government of the United States, based upon just and substantial grounds, for the maintenance of a government adequate for the protection of life and property and individual liberty and adequate for discharging the obligations with respect to Cuba imposed by the Treaty of Paris on the United States.'

"I believe that a continuous and thorough study of Cuban economic and political conditions should be made, so that the mission can be in a position at all times to give, when desired and without obligation, unofficial expert advice and assistance to the Cuban Government, in order to help Cuba's progress. I do not believe that there is any right or duty to go further than this, save in the case of the complete breakdown of the Cuban Government or in case of foreign aggression."

In a personal conference with the Secretary, this position was generally approved, and in the following month Secretary Stimson announced to the press that the United States was observing the Root interpretation of the Platt Amendment in Cuba.

In spite of a strict adherence to this policy thereafter, the attitude of the United States toward Cuba was misconstrued, as has been indicated. This misconstruction followed the lines of a widely accepted opinion once stated by Raymond L. Buell, as follows:

"Although the interpretation by the United States of the Platt Amendment has varied, one principle seems to stand out as a result of the last thirty years; namely, that the United States is 'opposed unalterably to any attempt which may be made to replace by violence or revolution the process of government'." [16]

The policy of absolute impartiality and non-interference during the revolution of August, 1931, is a contradiction to that generally accepted viewpoint. During the revolution, the United States Government did not even place an embargo on munitions of war entering Cuba. It was suggested that our Government do so, and such an act would have been properly within our rights under the usages of international law. The Cuban Government desired the embargo not so much because of its military value, but

[16] *Cuba and the Platt Amendment*, Foreign Policy Association, New York, April 17, 1929.

because of the moral effect of United States support.

Despite this non-partisanship, the position of the American Embassy became more and more difficult as the political bitterness and the economic depression in Cuba increased. In my opinion the events of these years during the second Machado administration are of too recent occurrence to permit full discussion by a former diplomatic officer. In accordance with the practice of the Department of State, many of the official reports of the period will be published after an adequate lapse of time and will no doubt prove enlightening to a public opinion that is as yet inadequately and at times inaccurately informed.

Suffice it to say that at the beginning of 1932 the Cuban situation underwent a definite change. For a year and a half Cuba had been in a state of disorder, with frequent bombings and assassinations, and with the jails intermittently filled with political prisoners. The previous August, President Machado had vigorously suppressed an attempted revolution, and had subsequently appeared to lose interest in making any concessions to the opposition. The effect of this upon the Embassy's position can perhaps be indicated by one paragraph from a despatch which I sent to the Department of State in January, 1932:

"At present we are no longer faced with the problem of an intransigent opposition unwilling to accept reforms and only intent on revolution, but we confront the question of the consequences of a Government intent on perpetuating an unpopular grip on the country. Machado, by renouncing his policy of conciliation and reform in his September message to Congress and by his other acts, has clearly served notice that he is no longer seeking to return to normal constitutional government in the Latin American sense of the term, but to extend his dictatorship. Our policy has been that of non-interference in Cuba's internal affairs. This policy was not understood at the beginning and the United States has been accused of supporting Machado and maintaining him in power. Although there is no justification for this accusation, the propaganda carried on by the Opposition, the 'claim racketeers,' and by Machado himself, as well as the shadow of the United States Government's policy in the past, undoubtedly have been the cause of widespread belief that Machado has our support. Our strictly impartial attitude during the revolution, as well as the persistent efforts of the Embassy to dispel this false opinion, have to a great extent recently modified this impression in Cuba, although it still persists, I believe, abroad."

PART VI

REVISION OF THE TREATIES

THE political, financial and economic situation in Cuba became progressively worse. Cuba again sorely needed the assistance of the United States. Our treaty obligations, strictly interpreted, imposed upon us a policy of non-interference, but in view of the many and various applications of the Treaty historically, the Cubans inevitably regarded this policy with skepticism. Our refusal to interfere with the Machado Government was interpreted as support of that Government. Our hands-off policy in the revolution of August, 1931, was insufficient to counterbalance the effect of former inconsistencies.

We were placed in an extremely and unnecessarily difficult diplomatic position. As early as January, 1932, we could report that "the faith of the Cuban people in the ability and disposition of the President to restore moral peace has been wholly lost;" we could acknowledge the futility of further efforts to persuade the Cuban Government, by appeal to enlightened self-interest, to reëstablish moral peace through political reform; and we could anticipate the inevitable collapse of the régime; but our policy did not permit us to take preventive action.

I felt a conviction that had been growing in the past years that the difficulty in our relations with Cuba was not to be found in the policy that we were then pursuing, which was less objectionable than any other that we might follow or that had been followed under the Permanent Treaty. The difficulty was with the Treaty itself. In a despatch on the subject on January 20, 1933, I said in reference to our policy:

"In reviewing in my mind the events of this (present) period and in comparing them with the history of our relations with Cuba from 1909 to 1929, I have come to the conclusion that the Cuban Government responds to friendly suggestions, not backed by direct official pressure, only when one of the following conditions is present:

"1. When it fears that failure to respond will result in intervention by the United States under Article III of the Permanent Treaty;

"2. When it is seeking a foreign loan for which it must secure the approval or acquiescence of the Government of the United States;

"3. When it fears that the Cuban opposition party is strong enough to oust it from power, but hopes that the adoption of reforms may placate the opposition or enlist the support of the Government of the United States.

"Numerous historical examples could be cited in support of these conclusions, but I believe it will be sufficient to recall the experience of the late General Crowder who undoubtedly commanded the respect, admiration and affection of the Cuban people to a degree greater than any other representative of the United States in Cuba. Despite his wide knowledge of Cuban conditions and his undoubted influence upon the Cuban government, his friendly and expert advice apparently was followed only under one or more of the three conditions just laid down."

I ventured the conclusion that this experience would be found to recur again and again, regardless of the particular individuals involved, and in view of these facts, added:

"The continuance of the policy does not commend itself as a thorough, progressive or final solution of the Cuban problem. It does not itself remedy existing conditions in Cuba, and because of its misinterpretation, the Cubans do not feel wholly free to demonstrate their own capacity to do so."

It, therefore, became my conviction that we should voluntarily offer to negotiate a new Political, as well as a new Commercial Treaty. I recommended, however, that the conclusion of these new treaties should be made contingent upon certain constitutional reforms and the reëstablishment of truly representative government in Cuba. This, of course, meant interposition in Cuban affairs, but under circumstances that would have been fully justified as an exceptional measure, and "the United States would have the satisfaction of again starting Cuba on the road to democratic government, but this time only after disposing of an obligation that is both irksome to Cuba and useless, if not actually harmful, to the United States."

Such effective action on the part of our Government would have been welcomed in Cuba and in other Latin American countries. The Cubans felt, with some justification, that the United States had exercised a paternal supervision over Cuba at various times in the name of humanity and in the interest of law and order. They believed that by the same token the United States once again should make representations to the Cuban Government for the protection of Cuban life and liberty, in view of the breakdown of constitutional processes. If such representations were coupled, as I believed and recommended they should be, with a voluntary suggestion to negotiate new treaties, they would be twice blessed.

In my despatch of recommendation, mindful of the imminent change in administration in the United States, I said:

"I am aware also that the modification of the treaty suggested above represents a drastic departure in our relationship with Cuba which, even though you might approve in principle, you might perhaps feel could not propitiously be inaugurated at this time. I feel none the less compelled to draw it to your attention, reiterating in conclusion my conviction that if we are to follow the Root interpretation and not to intervene in the internal affairs of Cuba, it would be better to adopt a more progressive policy in our relations with that country by modifying the Permanent Treaty. On the other hand, if we are ever to abandon the Root interpretation of the treaty for more active interest in Cuban affairs, good faith to Cuba should compel us to do so now."

There is, of course, one alternative to the modification suggested above, and that is a reënforcement of the Treaty to permit a close, compelling and final supervision over Cuban affairs, supported by armed intervention whenever necessary. This policy would seem to be in violation of Cuba's rights as a sovereign state and of both the letter of the Permanent Treaty and its spirit as interpreted by Secretary Root.

In addition to the injustice involved, interference with the normal affairs of a Cuban Government would seem to be definitely unwise. Under such a policy the American Embassy would become dictator of Cuba. Granted that this dictatorship might be benevolent and altruistic, it would not be omniscient, and in fact there is every reason to believe that it would not be able to cope adequately with Cuban problems. If we dictate to the Cuban Government, we must accept responsibility for the results of our dictation, which may lead to situations far beyond the capabilities of the mission.

For example, if, inspired by our own traditions and institutions, we dictate a policy of freedom of speech in Cuba, we would have to accept the responsibility of deciding when free speech becomes seditious; and we become responsible for any anarchy that might result from this decision. If we are to dictate to Cuba in order to administer the island effectively, we should occupy it outright. The Embassy would be unable to administer it. Armed intervention in Cuba as a result of carrying out this policy would undoubtedly be resented bitterly by an overwhelming majority of Cubans and Americans alike.

On the other hand, if in practice we are to avoid invoking Article III of the Permanent Treaty as a basis for exercising special supervision over Cuban affairs—if we are to intervene in Cuba only when such intervention would be justified and pursued under similar circumstances in other countries—we might well secure the benefits which would derive from the formal modification of the Treaty and avoid the evils resulting from our present undefined position. The inconsistency of our interpretation of the Treaty provides fuel for both Cuban and American abuse of it. Our relationship with Cuba is so intimate, and so ambiguous, that every omission or commission of the American Mission in Cuba, no matter how innocent, is invested with some deep political significance.

In spite of the unpopularity of the Platt Amendment since its inception, the Cubans have not hesitated to use it as a political weapon of their own. The two edges of this sword as wielded by the Cubans can be graphically demonstrated by reference to two paradoxical comments of the American Minister to Cuba in 1912 and 1913. On November 5, 1912, he telegraphed the Department of State, in connection with the victory of the Conservatives that year, that the Department must be prepared for an outbreak any day, since the Liberals refused to accept the result and said they *preferred American intervention to a Conservative victory*. On March 31, 1913, he stated in a despatch: "There is scarcely a Cuban with political aspirations who would dare to come out openly with expressions of friendship for the United States."

These apparently contradictory statements are an indication of what has happened under the Platt Amendment. It is publicly denounced, secretly utilized. Candidates for office have always been able to rally popular support by standing on a platform of Cuban nationalism, advocating the abrogation of the Permanent Treaty.

The distinguished jurist Cosme de la Torriente has said:

"In principle, an individual who has attained his majority and the full enjoyment of civil and political rights cannot be given a guardian to watch his steps and correct his mistakes—the individual in question grows accustomed to such guardianship and ends by being unable to do anything by himself. But, in practice, the right of intervention tends to embitter political struggle and furnish occasion for disturbances of the public peace. Certain people will always be found disposed to appeal to the foreign power, alleging that their lives are in danger, their property insecure, their liberties disregarded. If such appeals come from citizens of the intervening power, some attention may be paid to their complaints, and threats or protests may follow on grounds which are either well or badly taken. But if they come from nationals of the weaker country, no attention will ever be paid to them. At the most their petition will be published in the press, and their situation made more difficult than it was before." [1]

No doubt some American citizens with large investments in Cuba would vigorously oppose modification of the Permanent Treaty. They would probably assert that their investment in Cuba had been made in reliance upon the Treaty and in the belief that in Cuba they would receive from their own government a special protection which would not be extended to them in other countries. This theory, although supported by certain past precedents, seems to rest upon a mistaken and unofficial interpretation of the Treaty. Under any circumstances, present and prospective investors would no doubt welcome a clear understanding of the relationship between the United States and Cuba.

In negotiating a new Treaty, we should assume that Cuba must work out her own salvation regardless of the mistakes that she may make. I am in complete agreement with the dictum that it is far better for Cuba to make her own mistakes than to have our Government make mistakes for her. Our relationship with Cuba, insofar as the special protection of the lives and property of American citizens is concerned,

[1] "The Platt Amendment," *Foreign Affairs*, April, 1930, p. 364.

REVISION OF THE TREATIES 243

is and should be clearly understood to be similar to our relationship with other American republics under international law.

The special circumstances which influenced the device of the Platt Amendment at the close of the Spanish American War have no longer the force which they had at that time. We then felt a moral responsibility for the new State which we had brought into being. We felt the necessity for protecting the Spanish residents of Cuba from the anticipated reprisals of the liberated Cubans. At that time we had a real fear of foreign invasion in Cuba. And, finally, we must bear in mind that the draft of Article III, as enacted and in force today, is not the draft originally prepared by Secretary Root; the force of circumstances at that time compelled him to accept a change in phraseology which naturally modified his original draft, which was subsequently still further modified by his official interpretation.

In my opinion a number of changes in the Treaty would be advisable:

Our present treaty consists of eight articles, of which Article I reads as follows:

"The Government of Cuba shall never enter into any treaty or other compact with any foreign power or powers which will impair or tend to impair the independence of Cuba, nor in any manner authorize or permit any foreign power or powers to obtain by colonization or for military or naval purposes or otherwise, lodgment in or control over any portion of said Island." ²

This article, which has not been objected to by Cubans, should remain intact. It confirms a right which the United States by doctrine claims. It is essential to the preservation of the independence of a "country so small as Cuba, so incapable as she must always be, to contend by force against the great powers of the world." The Cuban Government in a note of February 9, 1912, had occasion to remind the United States Government of the need for protection. When France, England and Germany jointly made demands for claims of foreigners, the Cuban Government said: "If the Platt Amendment and the treaty in which it was embodied give the United States the right to intercede in our country in certain circumstances, those instruments likewise particularly impose upon it the obligation to defend us when those who are stronger than we menace us for reasons that are opinionable and debatable."

Article II reads:

"The Government of Cuba shall not assume or contract any public debt, to pay the interest upon which, and to make reasonable sinking fund provision for the ultimate discharge of which, the ordinary revenues of the Island of Cuba, after defraying the current expenses of the Government, shall be inadequate." ³

² U. S. *Foreign Relations*, 1904, p. 244.
³ *Ibid.*, p. 245.

This article imposes upon the United States Government a moral obligation which it cannot adequately meet unless it undertakes a thorough supervision of Cuban Government fiscal matters. This is impracticable and undesirable. The difficulties of administration are illustrated by numerous attempts of Cuban administrations to evade Article II in the past and by the fact that on several occasions it has been successfully circumvented by the general accumulation of large floating indebtedness in a time of inadequate revenues. In addition, the assumption of any public debt by the Cuban Government, in the absence of objection by the United States, leads to the erroneous inference that the United States guarantees that the ordinary Cuban revenues are sufficient to pay the interest and amortization. As previously stated, the bankers' advertising circular for the $50,000,000 loan of 1923 carried the following notice:

"Issued with the acquiesence of the United States Government under the provisions of the Treaty dated May 22, 1903."

Article II might well be eliminated from a new treaty, but in fairness to those who have purchased Cuban Government securities on the basis of that article, there should be a provision in the new treaty which would afford some protection for the holders of these securities until they are redeemed or refunded.

Article III reads:

"The Government of Cuba consents that the United States may exercise the right to intervene for the preservation of Cuban independence, the maintenance of a government adequate for the protection of life, property, and individual liberty, and for discharging the obligations with respect to Cuba imposed by the Treaty of Paris on the United States, now to be assumed and undertaken by the government of Cuba." [4]

The history of our relations with Cuba indicates that the utility of this article is outworn and that it is now inappropriate. In spite of a policy by the United States of strict non-interference in Cuban affairs, the existence of this article contributes to the ever-present threat that intervention may be deliberately provoked. In place of it might be substituted a guarantee of Cuban independence similar to that contained in the Treaty of 1903 between the United States and Panama.

Article IV reads:

"All acts of the United States in Cuba during its military occupancy thereof are ratified and validated, and all lawful rights acquired thereunder shall be maintained and protected." [5]

[4] *Idem.*
[5] *Idem.*

REVISION OF THE TREATIES

This article should be eliminated as it has lost the importance which it had for some years after the termination of the United States military occupation.

Article V reads:

"The Government of Cuba will execute, and as far as necessary, extend the plans already devised, or other plans to be mutually agreed upon, for the sanitation of the cities of the island, to the end that a recurrence of epidemic and infectious diseases may be prevented, thereby assuring protection to the people and commerce of Cuba, as well as to the commerce of the Southern ports of the United States and the people residing therein." [6]

This article was proposed by General Wood to assure a continuation of the sanitary plans of the military occupation, especially the fight against yellow fever. The article has out-lived its usefulness and should be eliminated from a new treaty:

Article VI reads:

"The Island of Pines shall be omitted from the boundaries of Cuba, specified in the Constitution, the title thereto being left to future adjustment by treaty." [7]

The "adjustment" has been made and therefore this article has no place in a new treaty.

Article VII reads:

[6] *Idem.*
[7] *Idem.*

248 THE UNITED STATES AND CUBA

"To enable the United States to maintain the independence of Cuba, and to protect the people thereof, as well as for its own defense, the Government of Cuba will sell or lease to the United States lands necessary for coaling or naval stations, at certain specified points, to be agreed upon with the President of the United States." [8]

The United States Government is now in possession of a naval base at Guantánamo in Cuba. When Article VII was proposed by the United States, Cuba feared that the projected naval bases might be used as points for watching over the domestic actions of the Cuban Government. This fear has been dispelled. There is a general recognition in the light of the history of the past thirty years, that United States occupation of a Cuban naval base is only in the interest of protecting both the United States and Cuba. This article should be modified to assure the United States Government perpetual use of adequate facilities at Guantánamo.

The final Article VIII provided for the ratification of the treaty.

. . . . .

The Reciprocity Treaty, governing commercial relations between Cuba and the United States, has been in force for thirty years. During that time, great economic and social changes have taken place in both countries. This Treaty should be adjusted in the light

[8] *Idem.*

of past experience to meet more satisfactorily the present commercial needs of the two countries. Without attempting here a detailed analysis of the products exchanged between Cuba and the United States and of the tariff schedules imposed upon them, we can lay down certain principles. Cuba's peaceful progress, in fact, her very life, is dependent upon sugar. In the interest of Cuba, in the interest of the 126 million consumers of sugar in the United States, and in the interest of the United States exporter who will benefit from the island's greater purchasing power, Cuba should be granted a fair quota of the United States sugar consumption and an effective reduction in tariff rates.

Cuba's social development has come to require adequate diversification of her crops, and her economic life has become more dependent upon crops other than sugar, as the United States has restricted its sugar market more and more to its own domestic island sugars. Taking this into consideration, Cuba should adjust her tariffs so that Cuban consumers will purchase from the United States whatever cannot be economically produced on the island. And, finally, the new treaty should include adequate and complete protection to American business interests in Cuba from the difficulties which have been encountered in the past. During the life of the Reciprocity Treaty, Cuba has enjoyed a favorable trade balance with the United States of over two billions of dollars. She will undoubtedly continue to enjoy large favorable balances. In return, she must make her adequate contributions for the proper and just protection of the commercial interests of the United States.

Senator Platt predicted that the Platt Amendment would "settle" the Cuban problem. It did not do so. Similarly, modification of it will not "settle" all Cuban difficulties; but it will, in my opinion, remove the most serious obstacle to better relations between Cuba and the United States. It will inaugurate a new phase in our Cuban problem that should be the harbinger of an era of amity and prosperity in the relations between the two countries, so closely connected by nature and mutual interest.

By a modification of the Permanent Treaty we can make a most important contribution to the development of Cuba's self-reliance. Also we shall finally fulfill our pledge recorded in the joint resolution of the United States Congress of April 20, 1898:

"That the United States hereby disclaims any disposition or intention to exercise sovereignty, jurisdiction, or control over said island except for the pacification thereof, and asserts its determination when that is accomplished to leave the government and control of the island to its people."

SELECTED BIBLIOGRAPHY

ACADEMIA DE LA HISTORIA DE CUBA. *Colección de documentos.* 8 vols. Habana: Rambla, Bouza y Ca., 1928–1932.

American Secretaries of State and Their Diplomacy. 10 vols. New York: Alfred A. Knopf, 1927–1929.

ARANGO Y PARREÑO, FRANCISCO DE. *Obras.* 2 vols. Habana: Howson y Heinen, 1888.

ATKINS, EDWIN F. *Sixty Years in Cuba: Reminiscences.* Cambridge, Mass.: Riverside Press, 1926.

BARBARROSA, ENRIQUE. *El Proceso de la República . . . bajo el gobierno, de J. E. Palma y J. M. Gomez.* Habana, 1911.

BONSAL, STEPHEN. *The Real Condition of Cuba Today.* New York: Harper & Brothers, 1897.

BUELL, RAYMOND LESLIE. *Cuba and the Platt Amendment,* Foreign Policy Association Information Service, New York. Vol. V, No. 3 (Apr. 17, 1929).

BUSTAMANTE, RAMÓN. *Cuba, the Pearl of the Antilles.* St. Louis, Mo.: Foreign Publishing Co., 1916.

CABRERA, RAIMUNDO. *Mis malos tiempos.* Habana, 1920.

CALDWELL, ROBERT G. *The López Expeditions to Cuba, 1848–1851.* Princeton: Princeton University Press, 1915.

CALLAHAN, JAMES M. *Cuba and International Relations: A Historical Study in American Diplomacy.* Baltimore: The Johns Hopkins Press, 1899.

Canini, I. E. *Four Centuries of Spanish Rule in Cuba.* Chicago, 1898.

Carbonell, José Manuel (ed.). *Evolución de la cultura cubana, 1508–1920.* 18 vols. Havana, 1928.

——— *Las Bellas Artes en Cuba.* Habana: El Siglo XX, 1928.

Carlisle, Calderón. *Reports to E. Dupuy de Lôme.* 2 vols. Washington: 1896–1897.

Casanova, Arthur Y. *Cuba y sus gobernantes, con motivo de la renovación de los poderes públicos.* Habana, 1917.

Chapman, Charles E. *A History of the Cuban Republic: A Study in Hispanic American Politics.* New York: The Macmillan Co., 1927

Cisneros Betancourt, Salvador. *Voto particular contra el proyecto de lotería nacional.* Habana, 1909.

Clark, William J. *Commercial Cuba: A Book for Business Men.* New York: Charles Scribner's Sons, 1898.

Collazo, Enrique. *Los Americanos en Cuba.* 2 vols. Habana: C. Martinez y Ca., 1905.

Coolidge, Louis A. *An Old-Fashioned Senator; Orville H. Platt, of Connecticut: The Story of a Life Unselfishly Devoted to the Public Service.* New York: G. P. Putnam's Sons, 1910.

Coster, Alfred. *The Literary History of Spanish America.* New York: The Macmillan Co., 1928.

Cuban Society of International Law, Havana. *Statements and Documents Relative to the Isle of Pines Treaty Between the United States and Cuba.* Washinging, D. C.: National Capital Press, Inc., 1925.

Davey, Richard P. B. *Cuba Past and Present.* New York: Charles Scribner's Sons, 1898.

Davis, Richard H. *Cuba in War Time.* New York: R. H. Russell, 1897.

SELECTED BIBLIOGRAPHY 253

Delmonte Y Aponte, Domingo. *Escritos de Domingo del Monte.* 2 vols. Habana: Cultural, S. A., 1929.

Dollero, Adolfo. *Cultura cubana.* Habana, 1916.

Duque, Matías. *Nuestra Patria: Lectura para hombres.* Habana: J. L. Gonzalez, 1928.

Ettinger, Amos A. *The Mission to Spain of Pierre Soulé.* New Haven, Conn.: Yale University Press, 1932. (London: Oxford University Press, 1932).

Ewart, Frank C. *Cuba y las costumbres cubanas.* Boston and New York: Ginn & Co., 1919.

Ferrara, Orestes. *El Pan americanismo y la opinión europea.* Editorial Le Livre Libre: Paris, 1930.

——— *Tentativas de Intervención Europea en América, 1896–1898.* Editorial Hermes: Habana, 1933.

Fewkes, J. Walter. *Prehistoric Culture of Cuba,* in "American Anthropologist", Vol. VI, N. S., No. 5 (Oct.-Dec., 1904).

Forbes-Lindsay, Charles H. A., and Nevin O. Winter. *Cuba and Her People of To-day.* Boston: L. C. Page & Co., 1928.

Freyre de Andrade, Leopoldo. *La Intervención gubernamental en la industria azucarera.* Habana, 1931.

——— *La Restricción de la zafra.* Habana, 1931.

Gallenga, Antonio C. N. *The Pearl of the Antilles.* London: Chapman & Hall, 1873.

García Kohly, Mario. *Política internacional cubana (Relaciones entre Cuba y España) y El Alma cubana a través de sus poetas (Dos días en Sevilla).* Madrid: B. del Amo, (1928?).

George, Marian M. *A Little Journey to Cuba and Porto Rico.* Chicago: A. Flanagan Co., 1930.

González Lanuza, José A. *Discursos y trabajos.* Habana: Rambla, Bouza y Ca., 1921.

Gower, Charlotte D. *The Northern and Southern*

Affiliations of Antillean Culture. Memoir of the American Anthropological Association, No. 35. Menasha, Wis., 1927.

GUERRA Y SÁNCHEZ, RAMIRO. *Historia de Cuba.* Habana: Librería Cervantes de R. Veloso, 1922.

——— *Un Cuarto de siglo de evolución cubana.* Habana, 1924.

GUITERAS, PEDRO JOSÉ. *Historia de la Isla de Cuba.* 3 vols. Habana: Cultural, S. A., 1927–28. (New York, 1865–1866.)

HAGEDORN, HERMANN. *Leonard Wood: A Biography.* 2 vols. New York: Harper & Bros., 1931.

HARING, CLARENCE H. *South America Looks at the United States.* New York: The Macmillan Co., 1928.

HARRINGTON, MARK R. *Cuba Before Columbus.* Indian Notes and Monographs. 2 vols. New York: Heye Foundation, 1921.

HAYES, CHARLES W., VAUGHAN, T. WAYLAND, AND SPENCER, ARTHUR C. *Report on a Geological Reconnaissance of Cuba.* Washington, 1901.

HILL, HOWARD C. *Roosevelt and the Caribbean.* Chicago: University of Chicago Press, 1927.

HILL, ROBERT T. *Cuba and Porto Rico, with the Other Islands of the West Indies: Their Topography, Climate, Flora, Products, Industries, Cities, People, Political Conditions,* etc. New York: The Century Co., 1898.

HOWLAND, CHARLES P. *American Relations in the Caribbean: A Preliminary Issue of Section I of the Annual Survey of American Foreign Relations, 1929.* New Haven, Conn.: Yale University Press, 1929.

HUMBOLDT, ALEXANDER, FREIHERR VON. *Ensayo político sobre la Isla de Cuba.* 2 vols. Habana: Cultural, S. A., 1930.

SELECTED BIBLIOGRAPHY   255

——— *The Island of Cuba,* translated from the Spanish, with notes and a preliminary essay, by J. S. Thrasher. New York: Derby & Jackson, 1856.
INMAN, SAMUEL GUY. *Trailing the Conquistadores.* New York: Friendship Press, 1930.
JENKS, LELAND H. *Our Cuban Colony: A Study in Sugar.* New York: Vanguard Press, 1928.
JOHNSON, WILLIS F. *The History of Cuba.* 5 vols. New York: B. F. Buck & Co., 1920.
JONES, CHESTER LLOYD. *Caribbean Backgrounds and Prospects.* New York and London: D. Appleton & Co., 1931.
——— *Caribbean Interests of the United States.* New York and London: D. Appleton & Co., 1929.
LAMAR-SCHWEYER, ALBERTO. *Biología de la democracia.* Habana: Editorial Minerva, 1927.
——— *La Crisis del patriotismo.* Habana: Editorial Martí, 1929.
LATANÉ, JOHN HOLLADAY. *The United States and Latin America.* New York: Doubleday, Page & Co., 1920.
LLAVERÍAS Y MARTÍNEZ, JOAQUÍN. *La Comisión militar ejecutiva y permanente de la Isla de Cuba.* Habana: El Siglo XX, A. Muñiz y Hno., 1929.
LLOYD, REGINALD. *Twentieth Century Impressions of Cuba.* London: Lloyds Greater Britain Pub. Co., Ltd., 1913.
LÓPEZ HIDALGO, AMBROSIO VALENTÍN. *Cuba y la Enmienda Platt.* Habana, 1921.
LOZANO CASADO, MIGUEL. *La Personalidad del General José Miguel Gómez.* Habana, 1913.
MACHADO Y ORTEGA, LUIS. *La Enmienda Platt: Estudio de su alcance e interpretación y doctrina sobre su aplicación.* Habana: El Siglo XX, 1922.

256 THE UNITED STATES AND CUBA

Márquez Sterling, M. *Las conferencias del Shoreham: El Cesarismo en Cuba.* Mexico, 1933.
Martí, José. *Hombres.* Habana: Rambla y Bouza, 1908.
——— *Ideario—Colección de Libros Cubanos.* Habana: Cultural, S. A., 1930.
——— *Obras reunidas por Gonzalo de Quesada.* 15 vols. Washington and Havana, 1900–1919.
Martínez Ortiz, Rafael. *Cuba: Los Primeros Años de independencia.* 2 vols. Paris: Le Livre Libre, 1929.
——— *General Leonard Wood's Government in Cuba.* Paris: Dubois et Bauer, 1920.
Matthews, Franklin. *The New-Born Cuba.* New York: Harper & Brothers, 1899.
Merino, Bernardo, and Ibarzabal, F. de. *La Revolución de febrero.* Habana: R. Veloso, 1918.
Millis, Walter. *The Martial Spirit.* Boston: Houghton Mifflin Co., 1931.
Morales y Morales, Vidal. *Iniciadores y primeros mártires de la Revolución Cubana.* 3 vols. Habana: Cultural, S. A., 1931.
Musgrave, George C. *Under Three Flags in Cuba: A Personal Account of the Cuban Insurrection and Spanish-American War.* Boston: Little, Brown & Co., 1899.
Ortiz Fernández, Fernando. *José Antonio Saco y sus ideas cubanas.* Habana: El Universo, S. A., 1929.
——— *La Decadencia cubana.* Habana, 1924.
Pardo-Suárez, Vicente. *Le Elección presidencial en Cuba.* Habana: Rambla Bouza y Ca., 1923.
Pepper, Charles M. *To-morrow in Cuba.* New York: Harper & Brothers, 1899.
Pérez, Juan de Dios. *Figuras nacionales.* Ranchuelo, Cuba, 1924.
Pezuela y Lobo, Jacobo de la. *Diccionario geográfico,*

SELECTED BIBLIOGRAPHY 257

estadístico, histórico, de la Isla de Cuba. 4 vols. Madrid: Mellado, 1863–1866.

———— *Historia de la Isla de Cuba*. 4 vols. Madrid: C. Bailly-Baillière (New York: Baillière Hermanos), 1868-1878.

PORTELL Y VILÁ, HERIBERTO. *Historia de Cuba, gráfica y sintética, en 101 cuadros, desde el descubrimiento hasta el Inicio de la República*. Habana: Cultural, S. A., 1932.

PORTELL-VILÁ, HERMINIO. *Narciso López y su época*. Habana: Cultural, S. A., 1930.

PORTER, ROBERT P. *Industrial Cuba: Being a Study of Present Commercial and Industrial Conditions, with Suggestions as to the Opportunities Presented in the Island for American Capital, Enterprise, and Labour*. New York: G. P. Putnam's Sons, 1899.

QUESADA, GONZALO DE. *Cuba*. Washington: Government Printing Office, 1905.

RAMOS, JOSÉ A. *Manual del perfecto Fulanista: Apuntes para el estudio de nuestra dinámica politico-social*. Habana: J. Montero, 1916.

RANDOLPH, CARMAN F. *The Law and Policy of Annexation, with Special Reference to the Philippines, Together with Observations on the Status of Cuba*. New York: Longmans, Green & Co., 1901.

Report of Provisional Administration. 2 vols. Havana, 1908–1909.

RIVERO, NICOLÁS. *Actualidades*. Habana: Cultural, S. A., 1929.

ROBINSON, ALBERT G. *Cuba, Old and New*. New York: Longmans, Green & Co., 1915.

———— *Cuba and the Intervention*. New York, 1905.

RODRÍGUEZ LANDEYRA, FRANCISCO. *Estudio sobre la geografía de la Isla de Cuba*. Zaragoza: La Derecha, 1896.

Roig, Enrique. *La Ley del dragado.* Habana, 1915.
Root, Elihu. *The Military and Colonial Policy of the United States,* ed. by Robert Bacon and James Brown Scott. Cambridge, Mass., 1916.
Rousset, Ricardo. *Historia de Cuba.* 3 vols. Habana, 1918.
Rowan, Andrew S., and Ramsey, Marathon M. *The Island of Cuba: A Descriptive and Historical Account of the "Great Antilla."* New York: Henry Holt & Co., 1897.
Rubens, Horatio S. *Liberty, the Story of Cuba.* New York: Brewer, Warren & Putnam, Inc., 1932.
Saco, José A. *Obras, compiladas por primera vez y publicadas en dos tomos por un Paisano del Autor.* 2 vols. New York: Libreria Americana y Extranjera de R. Lockwood é Hijo, 1853.
Sanjenís, Avelino. *Tiburón.* Habana, 1915.
Santovenia y Echaide, Emeterio S. *Huellas de gloria: Frases históricas cubanas.* Habana: El Siglo XX, 1928.
——— *Victor Hugo y Cuba.* Habana: Editorial Minerva, 1933.
Seligman, Edwin R. A., and Shoup, Carl S. *Informe sobre el sistema tributario de Cuba.* Habana: Carasa y Ca., 1932.
Stuart, Graham H. *Cuba and Its International Relations.* New York: The Institute of International Education, 1923.
——— *Latin America and the United States.* New York and London: The Century Co., 1928.
Suárez de Tangil y de Angulo, Fernando, Conde de Vallellano. *Nobiliario cubano; o, Las Grandes Familias Isleñas.* 2 vols. Madrid: F. Beltrán, 1929.
Terry, Thomas P. *Terry's Guide to Cuba, Including the Isle of Pines.* Boston: Houghton Mifflin Company, 1929.

SELECTED BIBLIOGRAPHY 259

Torriente y Peraza, Cosme de la. *Cuba en la vida internacional: Discursos.* 2 vols. Habana: Rambla, Bouza y Ca., 1922.

Trelles y Govín, Carlos Manuel. *El Progreso y el retroceso de la República de Cuba.* Habana, 1923.

U. S. Congress—Senate Committee on Foreign Relations. *Adjustment of Title to Isle of Pines . . . Report* (59th Cong., 1st Sess., Senate Doc. 2057). Washington: Government Printing Office, 1906.

―――― *Report of the Committee . . . Relative to Affairs in Cuba, April 13, 1898.* (55th Cong., 2nd Sess., Senate Rept. No. 885). Washington: Government Printing Office, 1898.

U. S. President, 1897–1901 (McKinley). *Messages of the President . . . on the Relations of the United States to Spain, and also Transmitting Consular Correspondence Respecting the Condition of the Reconcentrados in Cuba, the State of the War in the Island, and the Prospects of the Projected Autonomy.* Washington: Government Printing Office, 1898.

U. S. Tariff Commission. *The Effects of the Cuban Reciprocity Treaty of 1902.* Washington: Government Printing Office, 1929.

Valdés Domínguez, Eusebio. *Los Antiguos Diputados de Cuba y apuntes para la historia constitucional de esta isla.* Habana: El Telegrafo, 1879.

Valdés-Roig, Luis. *El Comercio exterior de Cuba y la Guerra Mundial.* Habana: Avisador Comercial, 1920.

Varona y Pera, Enrique José. *De la Colonia a la República: Selección de trabajos políticos, ordenada por su autor.* Habana: Sociedad Editorial Cuba Contemporanea, 1919.

―――― *Por Cuba: Discursos.* Habana, 1918.

Vasconcelos, Ramón. *El general Gómez y la sedición de mayo*. Habana, 1916.

Velasco, Carlos de. *Estrada Palma: Contribución histórica*. Habana, 1911.

Williams, Mary Wilhelmina. *The People and Politics of Latin America*. Boston: Ginn & Co., 1930.

Wright, Irene A. *Cuba*. New York: The Macmillan Co., 1910.

——— *The Early History of Cuba, 1492–1586, Written from Original Sources*. New York: The Macmillan Co., 1916.

Wright, Philip G. *The Cuban Situation and Our Treaty Relations*. Washington, D. C.: The Brookings Institution, 1931.

——— *Sugar in Relation to the Tariff*. New York: McGraw-Hill Book Co., 1924.

Zaragoza, Justo. *Las Insurrecciones en Cuba: Apuntes para la historia política de esta isla en el presente siglo*. 2 vols. Madrid: M. G. Hernández, 1872–1873.

INDEX

Absentee ownership, 169
Adams, J. Q., first Pan American conference and, 7; on Cuba and Puerto Rico, 3–4
Adams, J. T., 32
Advisory Law Commission, 207
Agramonte, A., 58
Agrarian reform, Cuba, 149, 151
Air transportation, 116
Alacran, 31
Almodóvar del Río, Duque de, 51
Altruism, 60
Alvárez, Angel, 188, 189
American Ambassador to Cuba, 186; intercession for prisoners, 187
American capital in Cuba, 110, 112; investment, 113
American diplomacy, European indictment of, 18–19
American Embassy in Havana, 186; non-partisanship in 1931, 232, 233; position in 1932, 233; propaganda against, 187
Americans, attitude to Cuba, 58
Amnesty laws, Cuban, 163
Annexation of Cuba, 9; discussion, 30
Armed intervention, 239
Army Appropriation Bill, 74, 83

Bacon, Robert, 198, 202, 204
Baire, 30
Bankers, foreign, in Cuba, 121, 122
Banks, Cuba, 116, 122; loans to Latin America, 127
Beaupre, Minister, 210
Beet sugar, 134
Beet sugar interests, 104
Billikopf, Jacob, on the American Embassy in Havana, 186

Black republic in Cuba, fear of, 8
Black Warrior affair, 17, 18
Blanco, Ramón, 37, 38
Bola, 185
Breckinridge, J. C., 21
Bribery in Cuba, 115
Brooke, J. R., 54
Brookings Institution, 137
Bryan, W. J., instructions on preferential rights in contracts, 223; policy, 208, 211
Buchanan, James, 9; nomination for President, 21
Buell, R. L., 232

Callahan, J. M., 5, 14
Canning, George, proposal as to Cuba, 6
Capitalistic system, 169
Capote, Méndez, 85, 89; on the Platt Amendment, 92–93, 94
Carroll, James, 58
Carter, Burnham, vii
Censorship of newspapers, 175–176
Central Highway, Cuba, 118, 128, 129
Céspedes, C. M. de, 23
Chadbourne plan for sugar control, 140; appraisal of effects, 146; attack on, 141; campaign against, 142; Cuban people and, 144; defense of, 144; financing, 145; operation, 143
Chapman, C. E., on Cuban graft, 157–160
Civil War, U. S., Cuba and, 21; effect on our Cuban policy, 22
Claims racket, 180, 181, 190
Clay, Henry, on Cuba and Puerto Rico, 4, 6, 7

261

INDEX

Clayton, J. M., 10
Cleveland, Grover, 31; Cuban revolution and, 32; message to Congress on Cuba, 33
Colby, Bainbridge, 225; policy, 213
Colonial relations, 1
Colwell, Captain, 199, 200
Communications, Cuba, 116
Congress, U. S., Cleveland's message and, 34; Joint Resolution for Presidential powers (1898), 45; *Maine* sinking and, 42, 43
Coöperation, political reluctance in Cuba, 170
Corliss, Representative, 81
Credit, Cuban, 123, 126
Crowder, General E. H., 156, 225; Advisory Law Commission and, 207; Cuban Senate's protest against his policy (1922), 229; electoral code, 161, 164; memoranda to Zayas, 214; mission (1921), 213; on Article II, 225; policy of advice to Zayas, 226
Cuba, ix; aborigines, xii, 49; author's acquaintance with, ix-x; banking, 121, 122; banking house's comments on relations with the United States, 228-229; characteristics, xv; climate and situation, x, xi, 110, 155; Constitutional breakdown, 237, 238; debt, 51; economic development, 110 (see also Economic development); education, 56; factions and absence of a middle class, 49; financial crisis of 1920, 224; foreign possession, question of, 68; freedom realized, 99; immigration, 114; international trade, 59; Military Government, 53, 55, 59; National Bank, 123; occupancy by the United States, 52; political activities, 155-191 (see also Political activities); population, xiii-xv; Presidential elections, 159; prosperity, 113; public debts, 216, 244, 245; sanitation, 55, 94, 247; slaves and mixed elements, 50; social reforms, 55; Spain's relinquishment, 51, 52; ten years' war (1868-1878), 23-29; transportation, communications, finance, 116; wages, 114; working out her own salvation, 242
Cuba Libre, 51
Cuban Commission in Washington (1901), 103
Cuban Congress, immunity of members, 166
Cuban Constitution, 61, 62; fault of similarity to that of the United States, 66; Root's letter on (Feb. 9, 1901), 67-71; United States relations and, 64, 65
Cuban Constitutional Assembly, 67; disappointment at Platt Amendment's passage, 84; Report of Committee on Relations, 71-72, 73; Root's letter and its effect, 71-72
Cuban junta, 24, 25, 30, 47, 177; value, 178
Cuban National Lottery, 162
Cuban reciprocity bill, 106
Cuban Republic, 23; disorders, cause of, 160; treaty relationships of the United States with, 47
Cuban revolution of 1895, 30; character, 30-31; leaders, 49; United States sympathy, 31, 32
Cuban Senate, *Memoria* (1902-1904), 89
Cuban student movement, 149, 166; martyrdom tradition, 167; objective, 169
Cuban teachers, 56
Cubans, xvi; ambition, 119; characteristics, 54, 120-121; dissatisfaction with foreign occupation, 60; economic situation (1900), 111; intelligence and energy, 155; intercessions for, 187-189; landowners and reform, 151; martyrs, 46; misconception of United States obligations, 52; politics as a career, 119, 120; temperament, 173, 174
Cushing, Caleb, 28

INDEX 263

Dance of the millions, 149–151
Democratic Party, U. S., foreign policy under Fillmore, 14
Derby, Lord, 28
Des Moines, 204
Dictatorship, 239; loans as related to, 127
Diplomatic relations, 235; beginning, 100
Doheny, E. L., 173
Dollar diplomacy, 168
Duranty, Walter, 131

Economic development of Cuba, 110; beneficent results of American penetration, 130; increase of Cuban participation desirable, 130; United States influence, 110–154; United States responsibility for Cuba's sugar industry, 138
Education, Cuban, 56
Elections, Cuban, 160
El Morro, 99
El Nacional, 42
Embargo, 232
England and Cuba, 5, 6
Estrada Palma, Tomás, 159; commission for negotiating a loan, 217; election, 178; pardons, 165; Presidency, 99; public debt question, 216; request for war vessels (1906), 197, 199; resignation, 204; Squiers and, 194, 195
Ettinger, A. A., 16
European aggression, fear of, 4, 5, 6
Evacuation of Cuba by Spanish troops, 53
Everett, Edward, on tripartite guaranty to Spain, 13
Exploitation of Cuba, 58

Farming in Cuba, 117
Ferrara, Orestes, 230
Fillmore, Millard, correspondence under, 12–14; policy as to Cuba, 14, 15
Finlay, Carlos, 57, 58
Fish, Hamilton, protests to Spain over Cuba, etc., 25–29

Foraker law, 58
Ford, P. L., 2
Ford, W. C., 4
Foreign capital in Cuba, 112, 118, 119; criticism of, 114, 115; penetration, 116
Foreign interference, fear of, 4
Foreign relations, U. S. policy, 208
Fourth of July speech (1932), 148
France and Cuba, 5, 6
Free trade, 147
Frelinghuysen, F. T., on American citizens abroad, 184
Fuller, J. B., 29

Gómez, Máximo, 24, 99, 159, 162, 195; American troops and, 47; pardons, 165; Presidency, 207; protest against meddling (1912), 211
González, W. E., 223
Graft, Cuban political, 157
Grant, U. S., Cuban revolutionists' appeal to, 23
Guantánamo, 211, 248
Guggenheim, Harry F., 188; comments on United States policy (1933), 236–237; despatch recommending modification of Permanent Treaty, 238–239; Fourth of July speech (1932), 148; intercession for prisoners, 187; paragraph from despatch in January, 1932, on Machado, 233–234; policy, 230–232
Gullón, Spanish Minister, on the *Maine* sinking, 44

Hagedorn, Hermann, 57, 61, 86, 87
Harrington, M. R., xii
Havana, ix, xiii, xv, 110, 150; American Embassy, 186, 187; American warships, proposed visit of, to (1930), 181–184; hotels, 118; rejoicing at end of American occupation, 99; rumors, 185; struggle and cartoons against Platt Amendment, 85; student martyrs of 1871, 167; yellow fever, 57

Havana, University of, 167
Hawley-Smoot Tariff, 136, 139
Hay, John, 208, 217; letter to Squiers (1904), 218; treaty with Cuba, 100
Hayes, R. B., on Cuba, 29
Hoar, G. F., 80
Hoover, Herbert, policy as to intervention, 168; warning on loans, 124
Hopkins, A. J., 196
Huau, J. A., 34
Hughes, C. E., broad view of Article II, 225; instructions to Crowder, 214
Human relations, Latin *vs.* Anglo-Saxon feeling, 173

Immigration into Cuba, 114
Independence of Cuba, 45–46, 243, 244; declaration, 23; plans for, 9; Root on, 69
Industrial system, 148
Industries in Cuba, 116, 117
International law, 231, 243
Intervention, 192, 246; American policy after 1909, 207; armed intervention as alternative of treaty revision, 239; Cuban reaction to, 48; disfavor, 50; formal, 45; inconsistent interpretation of Article III by the United States, 192; justification for interposition in 1933, 237; "preventive" theory, 210; reluctance of United States (1906), 198, 205; Root's interpretation of Article III, 192, 193; second occupation of Cuba (1906), 197
Investments in Cuba, treaty revision and, 242
Isle of Pines, 76, 77, 247; assigned to Cuba, 78; citrus groves and truck farms, 78; Root on, 78

Jackson, J. B., 221
Jefferson, Thomas, on Cuba, 2
Jessup, P. C., vii
Johnson, Willis F., 24, 177
Joint policy among nations, 5

Jones, Grosvenor, vii
Juntas, 176, 178; activity in the United States and American elements employed, 179–180; boys and, 178–179; term, 178. *See also* Cuban junta
Jury trial, 173
Justice, 173, 174

Kansas-Nebraska Act, 20
Kendig, B. R., viii
Knox, P. C., 208; Cuban Ports Company and, 221–223; instructions to Morgan (1909), 219; negro revolution and, 211; note to Gómez (1912), 210; policy, 208; "preventive intervention" theory, 210

Labor in Cuba, 114–115
La Discusión, 85
Land crabs, 179
Lansing, Robert, policy, 212
Latifundia, 149
Latin America, 49, 67; loans to, 124
Latin American policy of the United States, 48
Latin Americans, gambling instinct, 171, 172
Lazear, J. W., 58
Learned, H. B., 21
Lee, Fitzhugh, 38, 39
Ley de fuga, 187
Lincoln, Abraham, 21
Littlefield, Representative, 82
Loans to Cuba, 60, 245; by American bankers, 125; crisis of 1920 and, 224; delicacy of the question, 128; false rumor regarding the author, 185–186; loan of 1904, 217; loan of January, 1923, 228; Menocal and the budget in 1921, 224–225; Menocal's request (1917), 224
Loans to Latin America, 124; bankers and American people, 127
Lôme, Dupuy de, 32, 33; on McKinley, 37–38; on the New York Junta, 177; private letter pub-

INDEX

lished, 39; reply to Sherman (1897), 36; resignation, 40
Loomis, F. B., 194
López, Narciso, 177; appeals for aid, 9; expeditions, 10, 12
Lotteries, governmental, 163
Lottery graft in Cuba, 162–163

Maceo, Antonio, 34
Machado, Gerardo, American capitalist's attempt to help, 181; pardons, 165; policy, 234; reforms urged upon, 171, 172; student movement against, 149, 169
Machado administration, 125, 126; American loans to, 128, 129; excesses, 159; propaganda during, 190; recent events, 233; student warfare, 167; tax report and, 154; United States and, 235
McKinley, William, concern for Cuba, 53; Cuban question and, 35, 36; message on Cuba (April 11, 1898), 44; message to Congress referring to intervention, 38
Madison, James, on Cuba, 2
Magoon, C. E., 165; administration of Cuba, 206–207
Maine, 32; author's reaction to news of sinking, 42; despatched to Havana, 38, 40; destruction, 40, 41; State Department and loss of, 43
Mañach, Jorge, on economic conditions in Cuba, 111–112, 119
Manila, battle of, 51
Marcy, W. L., 16; instructions to Soulé, 17; on the purchase of Cuba, 20
Marshall, John, 67
Martí, José, 30
Martínez Ortiz, Rafael, on Cuban attitude to Platt Amendment, 85; on the Constitution of Cuba, 66–67; on the Root document and the Cuban Assembly, 71
Martyrdom of Cuban students, 167
Martyrs, Cuban, 46
Materialism, 60
Mendieta, Carlos, 188

Menocal, M. G., 159; pardons, 165; request for loan (1917), 224; revolution of 1931 and, 170
Miami, Fla., 176
Military Government of Cuba, 53, 55, 59
Miller, Hunter, viii
Millis, Walter, 24, 35, 177; on Congress and Cleveland's message, 34
Monroe, James, 2
Monroe Doctrine, 1, 3, 63
Morgan, E. V., 204; report as to deal with United Railways, and instructions from Knox, 219
Morgan, J. T., 81
Morris Amendment, 106
Mosquitoes and yellow fever, 57

National Bank, in Cuba, 123
Naval bases in Cuba, 76, 90, 248
Negro revolution, 211
Negroes in Cuba, 8
Nelson, Hugh, 3
New York Journal, 39, 42
New York Junta, 177, 178
New York Times, 186, 189
New York World, 39, 42
Newspapers, American, and Cuban propaganda, 191; Latin American, 175
Non-interference, 235, 246
Nufer, Albert, vii

Occupancy of Cuba, 52
Oil business in Cuba, 117
Olney, Richard, 168; offer to Spain of mediation in Cuba, 32–33; on the Cuban revolution, 31
Organized charity, 174
Oriente Province, 53
Ostend Manifesto, 18, 20

Packing business, Cuba, 117
Palmerston, Lord, 9
Pan American Asylum Treaty of 1928, 190
Pan-American Commercial Conven-

tion (1927), 125; Hoover's warning, 124
Pan American Conference, first (1826), 7
Pan American Federation of Labor, 230
Pardons, Cuban, 163, 165
Paris, Treaty of (1898), 52
Payne, S. E., Cuban reciprocity bill and, 106
Permanent Treaty, Article I, discussion, 243–244; Article II, 128, 145, 192; Article II, discussion, 244–245; Article II, interpretation and application, 215–229; Article III, linked with Article III, 208; Article II, purpose as stated by Root, 215, 216; Article II, Zayas on, 227; Article III, 192, 205; Article III, as originally drafted by Root, 243; Article III, broad interpretation, 215; Article III, misinterpreted by United States citizens, 196; Article III, usefulness now outworn, 246; Article IV, 246–247; Article V, elimination advised, 247; Article VI, 247; Article VII, discussion, 247–248; Article VIII, 248; changes advisable, list, 243–248; Cuban dislike, 194; Cuban point of view (1911), 209; Cuban protests against various policies of the United States under, 229–234; difficulty with, 236; inconsistency of interpretation, 240; mistaken interpretation, 242; powers assumed by the United States beyond the Root interpretation, 229; Root's interpretation of Article III declared the true policy, 231, 232; unsatisfactory evolution of relationship under, 192–234
Philippines, 111
Pierce, Franklin, Cuban attitude, 15; Cuban problem, 18, 20
Pigeon shooting, 178
Platt, T. C., 74, 77, 78, 79, 83; letter to Cuban Committee, 91–92; prediction, 250

Platt Amendment, ix, 52, 250; Article III, 100; Article III, Cuban opposition to, 98; Article VIII, 100; Articles II and V, discussion, 93–94; Articles III and VII, proposed changes in, 94, 95; changes made, 77, 79; congressional oratory on it as amended, 80–83; Cuban acceptance, vote on, 98; Cuban Assembly and people, attitude to, 84, 85; Cuban Committee in Washington (1901), 88–91; Cuban politicians and, 195; Cuban report on, 92–93; departures from the Root interpretation, 208; formation, 74; interpretations, 95–98; official interpretation as established by Root, 87, 88; original reason no longer valid, 243; prologue, 61, 62; Root's and Platt's phrasing of the intervention provision, 79–80; text, provisions, 74–76; trade relations under, 101; two-edged sword in Cuban hands, 240; unpopularity in Cuba, 100; vote on adoption, 84; Wood, Leonard, on, 86
Plenty, starvation in the midst of, 131–132
Political activities in Cuba, 155; personal nature, 158; politicians' wish for all or nothing, 172; reluctance to coöperate or compromise, 170; three abuses, 161; United States' relation to, 155–191
Political corruption, Cuban, list of practices, 158–159; Cuban vs. American, 156, 157
Political refugees, 189, 190
Politics, a malady in Cuba, 156
Polk, J. K., plan for purchase of Cuba, 9
Polo, Admiral, 27
Ports Company project, 220–223
Post Office scandal, Cuba, 61
Presidency, Cuban, 159, 160
"Preventive intervention," 210
Propaganda, Cuban, 175, 176, 180, 184–185, 191

INDEX 267

Public debts, Cuba, 216, 244, 245
Public works program in Cuba, 128, 129
Puerto Rico, 3, 4, 111
Purchase of Cuba, question of, 17, 19
Putnam, Herbert, viii

Quesada, Gonzalo de, 202; letter of Roosevelt to (1906), 202–204; recognition of justice of American intervention, 206

Railroads in Cuba, 116
Reciprocity Treaty with Cuba, 107, 248; passage, 108
Reconcentrado policy, 31
Reed, E. L., vii
Reed, Walter, 58
Refunding of Cuban debt suggested, 126
Reid, Whitelaw, 36
Republic of Cuba. *See* Cuban Republic
Revision of the treaties, 235–250
Revolution of August, 1931, 232
Richardson, J. D., 3, 10, 33, 35, 38, 45
Riva, M. A., letter on appeals to the American Ambassador, 188
Rivero, J. I., 131
Roberts, López, 25
Robinson, A. G., 72
Roosevelt, Theodore, 86; ending of occupation of Cuba, 99; landing of troops in Cuba and, 201, 202; letter to Quesada (1906), 202–204; message to Congress on reciprocity, 103; Reciprocity Treaty with Cuba, 107, 108
Root, Elihu, 56, 196, 204; Cuba and, 53; interpretation of Article III of Permanent Treaty, 192, 193, 231; on Cuban relations (1901), 62; on Cuban trade, 59; on fears of European aggression in Cuba, 63; on the Platt Amendment, 86, 87; on the relationship that should exist between Cuba and the United States, 67–71; reciprocity with Cuba, 101–103; report on work in Cuba, 54–55

Sanitation in Cuba, 55, 94, 247
Santiago, battle of, 50; *Virginius* incident, 27
Schuyler, Montgomery, 31
Seligman, E. R. A., on tax laws in Cuba, 153
Sherman, John, protest to Spain (1897), 36
Shippee and Way, 37
Shipping, 116
Sickles, D. E., 25, 27
Sigsbee, C. D., 40
Slave question, 7, 8; Cuba and, 20, 21, 29
Social justice, 174
Soulé, Pierre, 15; appointment, 15; instructions to, 16; mission, 17
Spain, 4, 5; American relations during Cuban insurrection (1868–1878), 25–29; Cuban trade, 14, 30; reforms promulgated in Cuba in 1897, 38; relinquishment of Cuba, 51, 52; proposed sale of Cuba, 5; protest against invasion of Cuba, 11; tripartite guaranty of Cuba proposed, 12–13; war feeling toward, 41, 42
Spaniards, 118
Spanish American republics, plots, 6–7
Spanish-American War, 23; declaration, 45; peace terms, 51
Spanish Colonial Government, 45
Spanish pioneers, xii
Sparkman, Representative, 82
Spofford, F. P., viii
Squiers, H. G., 100, 216; letter from Hay (1904), 218; position as Minister, 193; report on Cuba's first general election, 1905, 195; Zaldo and, 193, 194
Stalin, Joseph, on confidence and credit, 130–131
Starvation in the midst of plenty, 131–132
Stearns, Foster, 13
Steinhart, Frank, 197, 198, 201

INDEX

Stimson, H. L., 185; statement of policy toward Cuba, 230, 232
Sugar, 30, 110; American ownership of Cuban properties, 143; Cuban efforts to control, 139; Cuban production, 133; market and price, 109; prices, 134, 139, 143; surfeited market, 131, 132; tariff and, 136; United States problem, 137; United States supply, 135
Sugar cane, 132
Sugar industry, 102, 105, 106, 116; agrarian reform as related to, 152; complex character in Cuba, 141; Cuba's dependence on, 133, 135, 249; Cuba's needs, 148; foreign bankers and, 122; World War and, 134

Taft, W. H., 204; proclamation to Cubans (Sept. 29, 1906), 204-205
Tariff, 147, 249; arguments pro and con in case of Cuba, 105; lobbies of Congress and (1901), 104; sugar and, 136
Taxation, Cuban laws, 153-154
Taylor, Zachary, proclamation (1849), 9-10
Teapot Dome scandal, 157, 173
Teller Amendment, 45, 52
Ten years' war in Cuba (1868-1878), 23-29; American relations with Spain during, 25-29
Tobacco, 108
Tobacco industry, 102, 117
Torcaza, 178
Torriente, Cosme de la, 78; on intervention and the Platt Amendment, 241
Trade relations, 249; Cuban campaign for, 103; Platt Amendment and, 101
Treaties, conditioned on reforms in Cuba, 237; Cuban feeling toward revision, 238; new political and new commercial advised, 237; revision, 235-250
Treaty with Cuba, 100. *See also* Permanent Treaty; Treaties

Turlington, Edgar, vii

Unión Nacionalista, 181, 188
United Railways of Havana, 219
United States, foreign relations, 208; policy toward Cuba, 235, 236; political corruption, 157
University youth, 167; Latin American, 167

Vacas gordas, 114
Varona, E. J., 46; on Cubans, 120
Venezuela, 127
Virginius incident, 26-28
Votes, traffic in Cuba, 160

Wages in Cuba, 114
Walsh, Thomas, and E. L. Doheny, 173
Warships, American, proposed visit to Havana, 181-184
Webster, Daniel, 8, 12
Weyler, Valeriano, 31
Wood, Leonard, 247; declaration of end of occupation of Cuba, 98-99; in Cuba, 53-54; letter to Roosevelt on Cuban sentiment, 85-86; on the Cubans and the Platt Amendment, 86, 87, 88; order for a convention to frame a Constitution, 61, 64, 65; Post Office scandal and, 61; trade relations and, 103; yellow fever and, 57
Woodford, S. L., 37
World War, Cuba and, 60; sugar industry and, 134
Wright, P. G., on the sugar problem, 137
Wynne, Cyril, viii

Yankee Imperialism, 168
Yellow fever, 54, 56-57

Zanjón, peace treaty of, 29
Zapata Swamp, 178, 211
Zayas, Alfredo, 156, 160, 195, 214; Crowder, correspondence with (1922), 226-227; lottery graft, 162; memoranda to, 214; pardons, 165

WAYNESBURG COLLEGE LIBRARY
WAYNESBURG, PA.